I0063272

APPRAISING BUSINESS OPPORTUNITIES

The Stratisquare framework

Appraising Business Opportunities: The Stratisquare framework by Robert Hughes.

Published in 2023 by Hughes Books, an imprint of Hughes Consulting Limited.

NZ Business number 9429038579288
UK Registered number 05067369

www.HughesBooks.Info

Alpha Edition

© Robert David Hughes 2023

This book is copyright. Apart from fair dealing for the purpose of private study, research, criticism or review, permitted under the Copyright Act 1994, no part may be reproduced by any process without the prior permission of the copyright holder and the publisher.

ISBN 978-0-473-61147-7 (Paperback)
ISBN 978-0-473-61148-4 (ePub)

A catalogue record of this book is available from the National Library of New Zealand Te Puna Matauranga o Aotearoa.

Contents

Introduction   1

The business opportunity   16
     Identify & summarise

Aims, resources & constraints   20
     Elaborate expectations

Place the opportunity   24
     The value network
     Market sizing
     Trends & their impact

Buyers & the friction they face   33
     Target buyers
     Customer journey
     Product attributes

Demand, alternatives & competition   42
     Competing products
     Target revenue
     Competitive threats

Production process   51
     Choosing an activity type
     Supporting capabilities
     Knowhow, systems & processes
     Leadership & key people

Suppliers & partners   67
     Contractual relationships
     Cost of systems & processes
     Costs of operating

Initiatives for a successful outcome   79
     Success & assumptions
     Revenue growth initiatives
     Capacity initiatives
     Success & mitigating risk
     Resilience & options

Financial budgets & value   91
     Financial budgets
     Financial reports
     Lifespan & value
     Discount rate
     Sensitivities & dependencies

Assessment of the analysis   104
     Realism of the plan
     Market-centric evaluation process

Key influences on the work   112

Glossary   113

List of figures

Figure 1 Depiction of some of the markets in which a business operates and the contributors to its value — 3

Figure 2 Focus questions applicable to each contributor of value added — 7

Figure 3 Focus questions and related contributor, units of analysis, and analytical tools of product scoping study — 9

Figure 4 Illustrative table of contents for a business proposal seeking funding for a new venture offering a new to market product — 10

Figure 5 Illustrative table of contents for a business proposal to gain support for a new product in a corporate setting — 11

Figure 6 The Stratisquare business planning canvass — 14

Figure 7 Representation of the facets as the faces of a 10-sided prism — 15

Figure 8 Considerations in crafting your opportunity statement — 19

Figure 9 Value network map showing market share and key players at two points in time — 27

Figure 10 Illustrative customer journey map — 38

Figure 11 Value-for-money indifference and demand curves — 44-45

   A Market with two competing products, A and B

   B Perceived market opportunity to offer product C (taking market share from product B)

   C Provider of product B responds by increasing its value-for-money (potentially cornering the entire market)

Figure 12 Taxonomy of activity types — 54

Figure 13 Questions to establish the candidate delivery and acquisition methods — 55

Figure 14 Capabilities and information flow diagram of a retail venture utilising the arbitrage-arbitrage activity type — 58

Figure 15 High-level capability, input/output diagram for retail venture — 59

Figure 16 High-level systems and processes, and requisite knowhow and other capacity to provide the requisite functionality — 62

Figure 17 High-level information and communications systems to support key information flows — 64

Figure 18 Decision tree of some factors influencing the selection of a contractual relationship for acquiring inputs — 70-71

Figure 19 Deriving the contractual types to acquire capacity — 73

INTRO-
DUCTION

0

Application

The process of working out how to exploit a perceived business opportunity is a journey of discovery made in the face of a lack of knowledge about the future outcome. A scoping business plan provides a way to prepare for uncertainty while keeping a direct line of sight on the prize. The high-level analysis in the scoping business plan is usually enough for start-ups to seek funding from early-stage investors and for corporate programmes to gain stakeholder support.

The central premise of the planning framework set out here is that the design of a business angle provides a way to match the characteristics of the perceived business opportunity, with the: aims, expectations and constraints on promotors of the venture; market context; and the nature of an appropriate production process. The framework described here provides a way to take these four sets of considerations into account.

Opportunities

Opportunities can arise in any element market.

A venture operates in at least five element markets, any, or any combination, can contribute profit to it. A depiction of these element markets that contribute profit is given in *Figure 1*. These contributors of profit are:

› Contributor 1 from product markets by providing products whose value-for-money is greater than alternatives.

› Contributor 2 from commodity markets by selecting a set of inputs to support a highly productive production process through economical purchase of those inputs.

› Contributor 3 from asset markets by making valuable scarce resources from a high productive production process delivering planned outputs.

› Contributor 4 from markets for other contractual obligations by providing risk mitigants to ensure that business plans are met, and strategic options to provide the resilience for on-going profitability. Matters of social and environmental impact of the business are addressed under this contributor.

› Contributor 5 from financial markets by enhancing business value by financial management.

An advantage of using this

characterisation of a business is to acknowledge that opportunities for profit can occur anywhere in a venture's activities, for example:

› Use of appropriate financial gearing (Contributor 5).

› Use of business continuity insurance to guard against unforeseen interruption to the operation of the venture (Contributor 4).

› Use of on-demand delivery as a distribution channel (Contributor 3).

› Use of logistics to fulfil customer orders directly from suppliers (Contributor 2).

› Sales processes that uncover new customers (Contributor 1).

Figure 1 Depiction of some of the markets in which a business operates and the contributors to its value

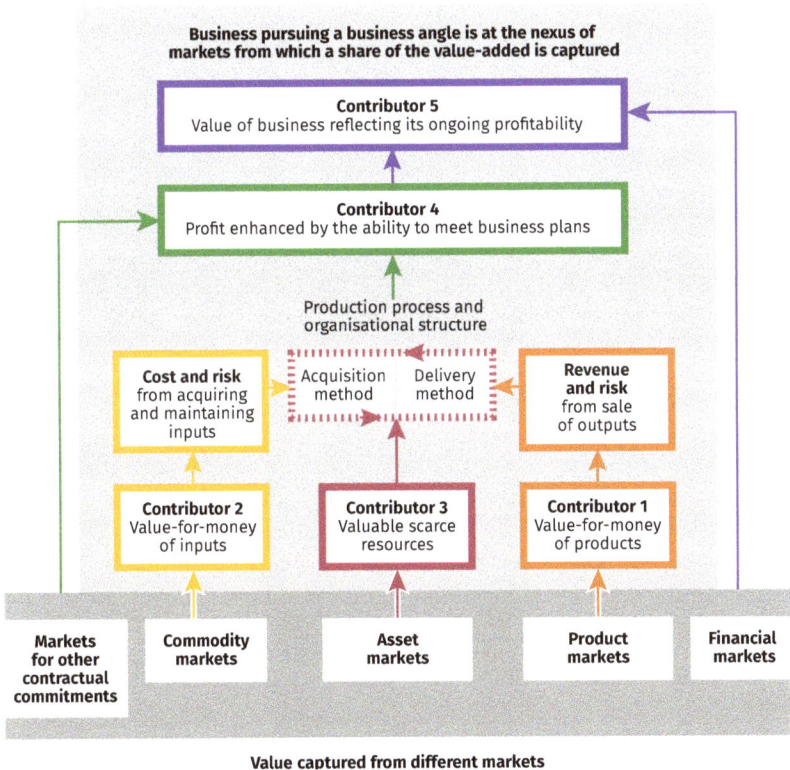

Business pursuing a business angle is at the nexus of markets from which a share of the value-added is captured

Contributor 5
Value of business reflecting its ongoing profitability

Contributor 4
Profit enhanced by the ability to meet business plans

Production process and organisational structure

Cost and risk from acquiring and maintaining inputs

Acquisition method   Delivery method

Revenue and risk from sale of outputs

Contributor 2
Value-for-money of inputs

Contributor 3
Valuable scarce resources

Contributor 1
Value-for-money of products

Markets for other contractual commitments

Commodity markets

Asset markets

Product markets

Financial markets

Value captured from different markets

Beware of analytic myopia

To start – a word of advice. Whilst the method of analysis presented in this guide can be replicated in a mechanistic way, an important feature of commerce is that opportunities are always in flux, and the assessment of the opportunity needs to continually keep up with, and be attuned to changes in the market. Analyses divorced from conditions on the ground and intermit knowledge of the production process to be used, are a major problem in business planning. A problem exacerbated by the longer the time between the market conditions summarised in the business plan and live participation in the market. Invariably people working in isolation of live conditions latch on the fad of the time, or groupthink, or belief that the planner has some special insight based on a superficial understanding of the available evidence. In contrast, continual interaction with customers where there are financial commitments to be entered, quickly synchronises participants in the value network.

The danger of analytic myopia is even more foolhardy when the assessment is undertaken by people who work in isolation from potential customers, partners, suppliers and other external stakeholders in the relevant element markets. As a rule of thumb, analysis undertaken by people more than two degrees removed from first-hand experience in a market should be treated as fiction. In the absence of continual incremental feedback, where by osmoses participants do not notice their drift with market trends, assessments of perceived opportunities must make a special effort to capture insights into how to make money from it. One way that this can be done is by learning from each step of the planning process and reworking each step, considering this new knowledge. Analytical efficiency is important and agility imperative. As is the need to guard against conjuring up an opportunity where none exists.

The framework presented here is practical and allows prior knowledge to be used to formulate the concept of the business opportunity, and then allows this to be revised by considering additional information from the analytical processes and market feedback. It is able to do this because the foundations of the analytical process are observable, external markets.

Planning process

This guide describes the first, scoping study phase of the three phases in developing a business plan. The scoping study involves setting down the big idea, what is wanted from it and the price to be paid for it. This phase culminates with the identification of the business angles available to exploit it, and the requirements to support it. The second phase is to discover the feasibility of making a profit by developing an initial, 'strawman' business model and the resources it requires. The third phase is to refine the design into a viable business model. There are other steps in the process of establishing a venture such as its legal form, sourcing finance, design of organisational structure, recruiting people etc. which are not described here as the focus is to work out the scope of the business angle in the first place.

In addition to articulating the opportunity, this planning process gives emphasis to: identifying how core competencies are to be created; and the intended actions to enable the venture to succeed, and the critical assumptions being made about what it will take for the venture to be a success.

Core competencies are a set of capabilities that contribute to the creation of profit, generally because of accumulated experience and knowledge, and/or investment in organisational wide systems. Core competencies are a scarce resource, along with control over rights to natural resources and information, and access in the form of patents, brands, and locations that attract people. Scarce resources are distinguished from other assets by their price being established by their profit earning ability. The competitive advantage enjoyed by a venture stems from scarce resources created, which are valuable, rare and difficult to imitate. The design of business angles that create core competencies is at the nub of the business planning process.

Business value, or simply value, in this context is Free Cash Flow (FCF) value. It is the net present value of expected profit over the planning horizon of the venture. The 'present value' is the value of a future amount today after considering the time value of money. The time value of money is called the

discount rate – frequently estimated as the prevailing interest rate available to the venture from lenders. 'Net' refers to the fact that the FCF value is the sum of the present value of expected profits for all time periods over a venture's lifetime.

A simple example to illustrate this, suppose a discount rate of 10 percent per annum, then an investment of $100 today will be worth $110 in one year's time and $121 in two years' time. By reversing this logic, if a business venture with a two-year lifespan is forecast to generate a return of $110 at the end of year one and $121 at the end of year two then its present value is $200. If $100 were invested today to generate that $200 forecast income, then the FCF value of the business is $100, being the present value of the income of $200 less the initial investment of $100, giving the net present value.

Scoping business plan

Coverage of the scoping business plan

Purpose

The purpose of the scoping business plan is to define the big idea in a way that there is some prospect of 'finding the money' with the available resources. The process to do this starts by summarising the perceived business opportunity; and then goes on to elaborate the capital, risk and return expectations from the venture. Against this backdrop, the next step is to place the opportunity in the value network for the relevant element market.

The opportunity placed in the value network is the epicentre of the scoping study. Considerations here are the structure of the value network, market context and market trends, and the speculation being undertaken to grasp the opportunity. From this point the analysis then follows two trajectories, first to explore the demand side characteristics. Coverage of the key players including the target customers in the relevant element markets, and the point of difference and value-for-money in the value proposition. The second trajectory is the supply side considerations covering the alternative activity types and corresponding business angles, the systems and processes to be used, and how core competencies are to be created.

Questions being asked

There is a direct line of progression from the initial idea through to its refinement in the business angle. The framework enables progressive refinement of the business angle so that it converges on a seam of value added, that meets the aims, expectations and constraints of the businesspeople involved. Coverage of each of the considerations in the analytical process is framed into a series of questions in *Figure 2*.

Facets 1–9 of the analysis are undertaken at a high-level with attention given to factors that impact the expected value of the opportunity. Qualitative assessments are used in this analysis where quantitative data is unavailable and to accommodate the uneven quality of information used in the analysis, Facet 10 considers the reliance of the overall findings on the assumptions, guesses and quality of information used.

The relevant focus questions covered in the scoping business plan are given in *Figure 2*. The table also shows the focus question where the perceived business opportunity relates to each of the contributors of value.

Figure 2 Focus questions applicable to each contributor of value added

	Contributors				
Facet	1. Products providing better value-for-money than alternatives	2. Productive and economical production process	3. High productive production process	4. Reliably meeting business plans	5. Enhanced business value
1	**WHAT** is the perceived opportunity and what are its key features?				
2	**WHAT** are the aims, expectations, resources and constraints on investment, return, and risk of loss?				
3	**WHERE** is the opportunity for profit in the value network given the macro trends?				
4	**TO WHOM** is the value proposition targeted and to what effect?	**WHO** are the suppliers?	**WHO** are the relevant contractual parties?	**WHO** are the owners and other key stakeholders?	**WHO** are the relevant external stakeholders?
5	**WHICH** are the competing products and their perceived benefits?	**WHICH** are the alternative solutions?		**WHICH** are the alternative options?	**WHICH** alternative ways are available?
6	**HOW** is the aim to be realise by using an activity type and capabilities?	**HOW** is the aim to be realise through procurement, the set of inputs and processes redesign?	**HOW** is the aim to be realise through system and process improvement and redesign?	**HOW** is the aim to be realise through systems, process, options and contracts?	**HOW** is the aim to be realise through financial engineering?
7	**HOW** much will it cost?				
8	**WHY** is a share of the value added available?				
9	And, its value?				
10	**WHEN** is the right time to pursue the business angle given the alternatives and macro trends, and available information?				

To illustrate the planning process, this application guide describes a new venture opportunity for a new product, and is therefore the application of the planning framework to Contributor 1. The framework set out here can be applied to opportunities in each of the contributors of profit, but the scope of the coverage at each of the facets will be determined by the nature of the contributor, and is applicable to evaluating the net benefit of an incremental change, project or standalone new venture.

The units of analysis used for the product (Contributor 1) focus questions and analytical tools are set out in *Figure 3*. The methods to answer each of the product focus questions are described in detail, in the order of the suggested sequence of analysis, in the sections following this introduction.

To place the focus questions into context, *Figure 3* also shows the contributor relevant to the focus question. Each contributor is related to at least one focus question. In addition, one facet relates to setting the market context for the opportunity (Facet 3).

Figure 3 Focus questions and related contributor, unit of analysis, and analytical tools of product scoping study

	Facet & Contributor	Unit of analysis	Analytical tool
1	Value-for-money product	Opportunity	Opportunity analysis
	Question: What is the perceived opportunity and what are its key features?		
2	Financial performance	Owners & other stakeholders	Analysis of aims, resources and constraint
	Question: What are the aims, expectations, resources and constraints on investment, return, and risk of loss?		
3	Markets	Market participants	Value network map Market size estimate
	Question: Where is the opportunity for profit, given the value network and macro trends?		
4	Value-for-money product	Buyers	Buyer needs Product benefits
	Question: To whom is the value proposition targeted and to what effect?		
5	Value-for-money product	Revenue	Value-for-money and demand curves
	Question: Which are the competing products and their perceived benefits?		
6	Core competency	Capabilities	Activity type matrix Capabilities and information flow diagram
	Question: How is the aim to be realise by using an activity type and capabilities and how much will it cost?		
7	Economical inputs	Costs	Suppliers and partners Cost structure
	Question: How much will it cost?		
8	Meets commitments	Gross margin	Gross margin Establishment programs
	Question: Why is a share of the value added available?		
9	Financial performance	FCF value	FCF budget Sensitivity analysis
	Question: And, its value?		
10	Financial performance	Time Uncertainty	Robustness of analysis and information gaps
	Question: When is the right time to pursue the business angle given the alternatives and macro trends, and available information?		

Having completed the analysis, the next issue is how to present the findings, and that is entirely situation dependent. To show this *Figure* 4 provides examples of the table of contents of a business proposal seeking funding for a new venture offering a new to market product, and *Figure 5* gives the table of contents for a business proposal seeking support in a corporate setting. A new venture seeking funding aims to sell its vision to prospective sponsors whereas in a corporate setting the scoping plan aims to marshal internal stakeholder support, and to do this must address matters of concern to these stakeholders.

Figure 4 Illustrative table of contents for a business proposal seeking funding for a new venture offering a new to market product

Contents	Supporting analysis	
Highlights – what we are offering investors		
About the opportunity	1	
The sector, its trends and our focus in the value network	3	
How we will carve out a place in the market	5	
Our aim and expectations, and limitations of our assessment	2	10
Financial budgets and funding requirements	7	9
Target buyers and demand	4	5
Benefits to buyers, the minimum viable product and market testing	4	
Alternatives and competing value propositions	5	
Our game plan to grow our position in the market and revenue	8	
Capabilities and organisational structure, and suppliers	6	7
Our plan to build capacity and costs	7	8
Strategies to deal with the risk, and our knowhow	8	
Leadership, key people and their accountability for creating value	6	8

Figure 5 Illustrative table of contents for a business proposal to gain support for a new product in a corporate setting

Contents

Contents	Supporting analysis	
Executive summary		
Introduction		
Link to business plan strategies	2	
The proposal	1	
The solution	4	
Options analysis	5	
Outcome/ benefit description	9	
Success criteria	3	
Assumptions and constraints	8	9
Dependencies/ linkages	6	
Business and process impacts	6	
Sustainability impacts	2	
Financial summary	9	
Major risk summary	8	
Project approach and key milestones	8	
Project governance and resource structure	6	
Appendix A Stakeholder consultation	2	
Appendix B Resource plan	8	
Appendix C Benefit profile	9	

Assessing the validity of the analysis

Part of the information incorporated into the analysis, is on the quality of the available information and why it is selected, and how it is to be applied in the analytical framework. Conclusions are drawn from the weight of the evidence available and the limits to this, in the form of the critical assumptions on which the findings rely. The overall assessment of the collected evidence used, and its limitations, is applied to reach conclusions at each stage of the planning process. In drawing attention to this, it is easy to see how partial information of uneven quality can also result in 'good enough' conclusions with caveats on the uncertainty involved which are still deemed acceptable to proceed to the next step. This point is emphasised because business plans are frequently grounded in a few handpicked pieces of evidence, that are presented in a way to exploit framing bias, and where in fact there is only a weak potential for their being a valuable business angle.

Applying an assessment process of this type helps reveal the uncertainty embodied in the business angle, providing the opening for the business model to put in place appropriate mitigants.

Undertaking this type of analysis is particularly valuable for short-lived, spontaneous opportunities where speed of response is of the essence. This is because in that type of setting, key parts of the business strategy are (1) to quickly get in to harvest value from the opportunity at hand, and then (2) to parlay into another opportunity or exit. As an aside, it is worth pointing out that excellence in the business binary (operational management of being able to build the systems and processes required to exploit a perceived opportunity, and marketing and sales to realise the opportunity) are as important as being able to identify the opportunity in the first place. There can be no other way.

While a sequential process is described for simplicity, its execution is not sequential, what is learned in each successive step should result in previous steps being revisited and reworked. To ensure that the analysis accords to reality the tests are applied at the end of each phase to assess the findings from the investigation. There are two reasons to be concerned that the analysis may not accurately depict conditions on the ground, the first is that sitting at a desk and staring at a computer screen brings isolation and detachment from what is happening on the street, and second, prolonged familiarity with analysis and championing of the worth of the business opportunity can cloud judgement leading to over enthusiastic evaluation of the opportunity and underestimation of operational and sales challenges. These tests are described in the last section, *Facet 10: Assessment of the analysis.*.

With prolonged and remote analysis of the business angle it is important that the result is a practical business proposition grounded in the available evidence and stripped of imagined paths to success. In a typical project scenario those working on the various aspects will enthusiastically champion their part and collectively the entire project. This enthusiasm can underestimate risks, particularly in implementation. This leads to under resourcing of implementation and operational phases. These risks can be addressed in two ways: first, **keep it simple** by ensuring that the production process chosen for the selected activity type, is as simple as possible, and second, **stay focused** by using the least own resources in the venture. These are both ways to help maintain a focus on the business objectives of the venture by using a minimum viable solution.

The Stratisquare

Overview

That a business operates in several element markets concurrently is represented in the business planning canvas in *Figure 2* – referred to as a Stratisquare. This depiction is used to structure the analysis supporting a business plan.

The Stratisquare provides a standardised format to communicate the idea of the business opportunity, and to show the analysis that has led to its development into a business angle, whose commercial feasibility and viability can then be evaluated. A business angle is a perceived business opportunity and activity type to exploit it.

Method

The Stratisquare traverses each of the 10 areas of focus, including the value proposition to identified buyer groups, points of difference to competitors, the cashflow profile and assessed value, and comment on the critical assumptions and overall confidence that can be placed on the findings.

The one-page summary is used in two ways. It is used to summarise and collate the findings from each area of analytical focus. These findings are on the challenges and features that can be leveraged and used as ways to overcome the key challenges and capitalise on positive factors. This is the key information that anyone should know about this potential business angle. This information is specifically used in *Facet 8: Initiatives for a successful outcome*. The one-page summary is also used as a tool for brainstorming, to clarify the idea of an opportunity, and to sketch out the business angle.

The opportunity is the central focus on the scoping business plan, and all other facets elaborate on how to exploit the perceived opportunity profitably. Revenue and costs are summarised on the righthand side. The resultant diagram organising and summarising the key information about the perceived opportunity is the Stratisquare.

Multiple views on the opportunity

Each facet provides a quite different perspective on the perceived opportunity. A 10-sided prism is a representation of how each facet provides a different perspective on the challenges faced in realising the perceived business opportunity. Each of these perspectives has its foundations in an observable market. *Figure 7* shows the net of a 10-faceted prism. This representation is used as a design element in this guide to reinforce that each facet provides new information on the perceived opportunity.

Figure 6 The Stratisquare business planning canvass

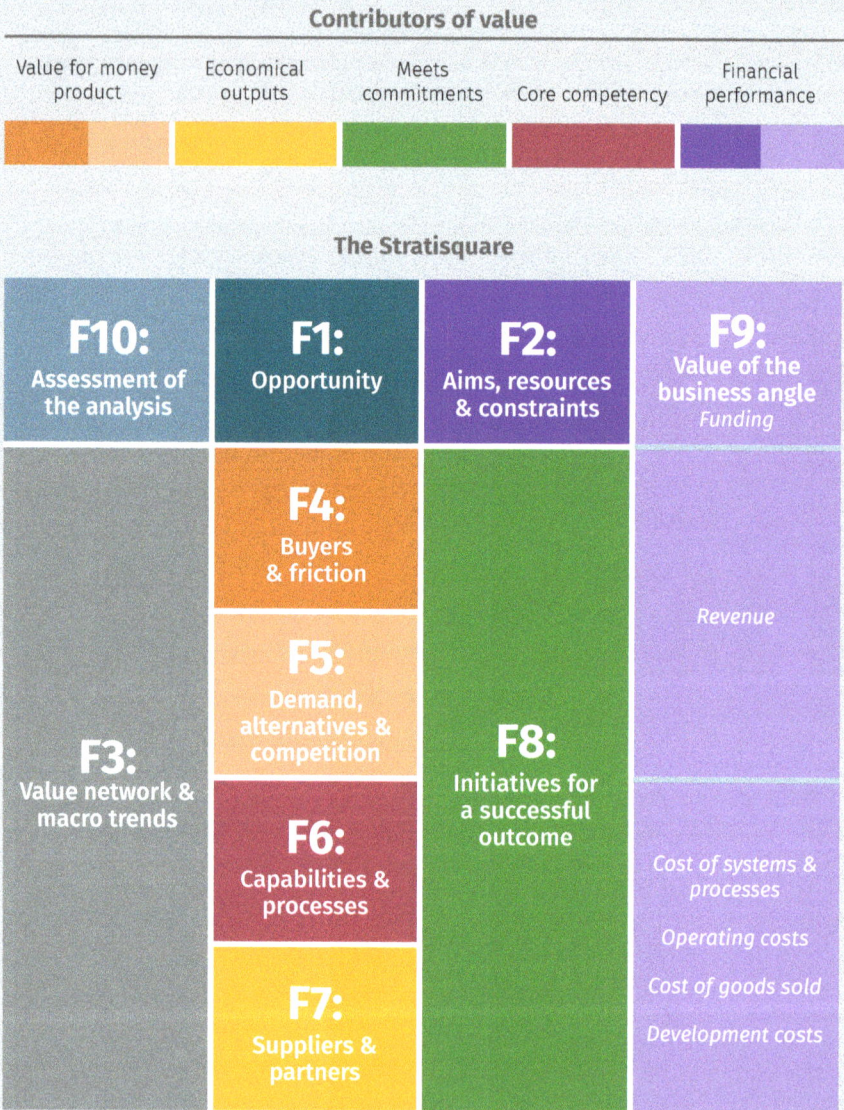

Figure 7 Representation of the facets as the faces of a 10-sided prism

Facets	
1	The business opportunity
2	Aims, resources & constraints
3	Place the opportunity
4	Buyers & the friction they face
5	Demand, alternatives & competition
6	Production process
7	Suppliers & partners
8	Initiaives for a successful outcome
9	Financial budgets & value
10	Assessment of the analysis

THE BUSINESS OPPOR- TUNITY

FACET

1

1

1.1
Identify & summarise

Overview

The inspiration for your perceived opportunity may come from anywhere — ideas for improving on an existing business venture, insight for a new branch of an industry, speculation in a new innovation, or any other intuition into a promising industry or business niche. Clearly identifying your business opportunity statement is the most important step in the scoping process.

Once the opportunity is identified, the focus then shifts to crafting it into a commercial business angle and this provides the launch pad for the next steps in the planning process. As you move through the process, this opportunity statement will be hwoned into a proposition designed to create value for your venture, so careful consideration of how to best articulate and frame it is essential.

In articulating the opportunity, it is important to keep two key perspectives in mind: looking forward to the future market, and looking backward to experience. There can be tension between these two perspectives and the available resources. This happens especially when there are legacy products and production processes which have too much influence on forming the business angle, therefore compromising the opportunity to innovate or create value.

Naturally, there are challenges with developing a clear opportunity statement (or businesses would never fail). These can stem from:

› *Identifying an opportunity based on a backward-looking view –* this is a 'here and now' vision based on experience in the recent past, but suffers from lack of insight into how to succeed as markets evolve

› *Amateur or superficial view –* trying to identify an opportunity based on inadequate understanding of the market

› *Narrow view –* the opportunity has been reduced to something too specific or niche to be viable

› *Wide view –* trying to include too many aspects or details in identifying your opportunity making it unwieldy and unmanageable

› *Biases* such as zeitgeist, patternicity and confirmation biases

Once these hurdles are cleared, the next step is to explore and understand the limits and impacts of the potential opportunity. After this, you can narrow the opportunity statement into a specific proposition. As you proceed through the scoping process and gain further insight you will use this to revise and refine the description of the opportunity.

Method

The statement of the opportunity describes a potential source of profit that requires serious attention. This statement is a few sentences in length. The rest of the description is its elaboration covering: the problem being solved or the need addressed by the opportunity, the solution or product to do this and its features, and the proposed benefits that will be realised from the opportunity.

The description of the opportunity should cover:

› the idea;

› the element markets involved;

› its scope in relation to a specific area of business or generic to a type of business;

› the degree the opportunity is derived from scarce resources and speculation; and

› how well the opportunity is understood, that is, the degree of knowledge possessed about the opportunity compared to other informed people.

A depiction of the opportunity analysis is given in *Figure 8.*

Figure 8 Considerations in crafting your opportunity statement

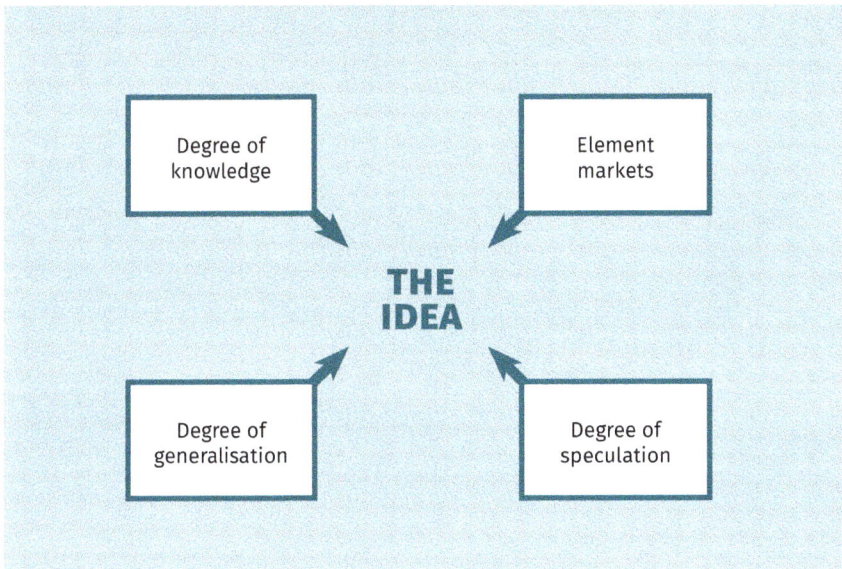

The coverage of the description of the perceived business opportunity:

› Opportunity:

  › What is the idea?

  › Which element markets does it relate to?

  › Describe the scope of the idea, that is it narrowly focused to a situation or generic to a type of situation?

  › What is the proportion of speculation involved?

  › How much is known about the idea?

› Product:

  › What is the problem being solved or needs being met?

› Who are the target buyers?

› How are the needs to be met or what product is to be provided?

› What is the product feature set?

› What benefits are to be realised by the buyer?

AIMS, RESOURCES & CON- STRAINTS

FACET 2

2.1
Elaborate expectations

Overview

At the outset it is important to clarify the price investors are prepared to pay to participate in the opportunity and what is wanted in return. One reason for being clear about the parameters around capital, risk, return and other expectations is because having identified an opportunity there is scope to select an activity type to align with these constraints.

Another reason for clarifying expectations is to plan into the project options to exit, be it because it successfully realises its plans (e.g. cashing up its value through sale, or seeking further funding for growth), or to wind up the venture in order to stem the losses.

Method

Getting clarity on these conclusions can be difficult even in a corporate setting. In many situations, the approach is to go along with the proposition until it becomes 'uncomfortable' without stating in advance what the limits are. It is important to clarify these issues as a means of counteracting any tendency for the proposal to gain a life of its own without proper scrutiny and squandering resources with no prospect of recovering them. It is also important to gain clarity on this so as not to be left in the lurch by 'fair weather friends'.

For business people a key factor is the requirement to shoulder risk and this should be done in such a way as to minimise its cost for potential loss. This can be done by being careful of the risk being taken on and assessing its expected consequences and cost of off-laying elements of risk through contracts such as insurance. For small businesses and start-up ventures, the magnitude of the risks involved is soon sheeted home by the guarantees that banks, suppliers and other providers of finance can require.

Also, relevant at the outset of an endeavour is consideration of the resources and capital available. A key resource is the knowhow and experience of the people working in the venture. The capital available is another important consideration that will shape the venture.

Information on this set of considerations can be elicited by the following questions:

1. Aim:
   › What is the aim of the venture?
   › How does this advance corporate strategy (where this applies)?

2. Return:
   › What is the magnitude of the return expected?
   › In what form is the return expected to take?
   › When is it to be realised?

3. Risk:
   › What type of risk and magnitude of loss is acceptable to be carried?
   › What risk mitigants are to be put in place and at what cost?
   › What level and type of risks are unacceptable (to clarify the acceptable return)?

4. Resources:
   › What resources are available, and under what terms and conditions?
   › What experience and knowhow are available in key people, and how are these to be used by the venture?

5. Commitment:
   › What loss is prepared to be suffered by the various stakeholders and over what period?
   › What is the limit to the commitment to creating a successful venture before stakeholders withdraw support?
   › When and under what conditions will stakeholders exit the venture?

6. Capital:

   › Who are the providers of funding?

   › What magnitude of funding is available and what are its terms and conditions?

   › What are the alternative sources of funds?

   › For providers of in-kind investment, how is this to be valued?

   › What are the conditions for the withdrawal of investment?

7. Control:

   › Who is to own the intellectual property rights created by the venture?

   › How much do the founders value control?

   › How important are strong governance arrangements to realising the aim?

PLACE THE OPPOR- TUNITY

FACET

3

3

3.1
The value network

Overview

Analysis of the value network aims to identify its key features and to explain changes in it driven by macro trends. Where the opportunity involves a market disruption, then it aims to explain how success of the venture could alter the future structure of the value network.

Method

The description of the value network sets out the background information in which to understand the business opportunity. The scope of the value network and its participants is dictated by the contributor of profit that the opportunity is related to. The analytical tool for this analysis is the value network map (see *Figure 9*).

The value network map provides a snapshot at a point in time, of the key participants and their relative market share. Customers are placed on the right-hand side of the map and providers (and in turn their suppliers) on the left-hand side. The map shows the allocation of market share between participants, and not the flow of materials and their transformation. In general, players further up the value network (further to the left) will have less control over the allocation of value between the parties but this is not always the case – the value controller could be several steps removed from the final customer.

Where relevant, at the boundary between stages in the value network, identify the market coordination mechanism. Market coordination mechanisms are the dominant contractual relationship used in exchanges between the parties – this is a topic considered in more detail in *Section 7.1: Contractual relationships*.

In competitive markets with no dominant players it is convenient to cluster players into groups based on the similarity of competitive behaviour at each stage in the value network. The number of stages depicted will consist of, at least, one stage on either side of the positioning in the value network being considered.

Considerations in placing the opportunity in the value network of the relevant element markets are:

› Who are the major players or categories of players covering buyers, competitors and suppliers, substitutes and complements related to the product?

› What are the relative market shares of the key players (from *Section 3.2: Market sizing*)?

› What are the market coordination mechanisms between stages in the value network (see *Section 7.1: Contractual relationships* and are there any special relationships between parties that are material to the analysis?

Figure 9 Value network map showing market share and key players at two points in time

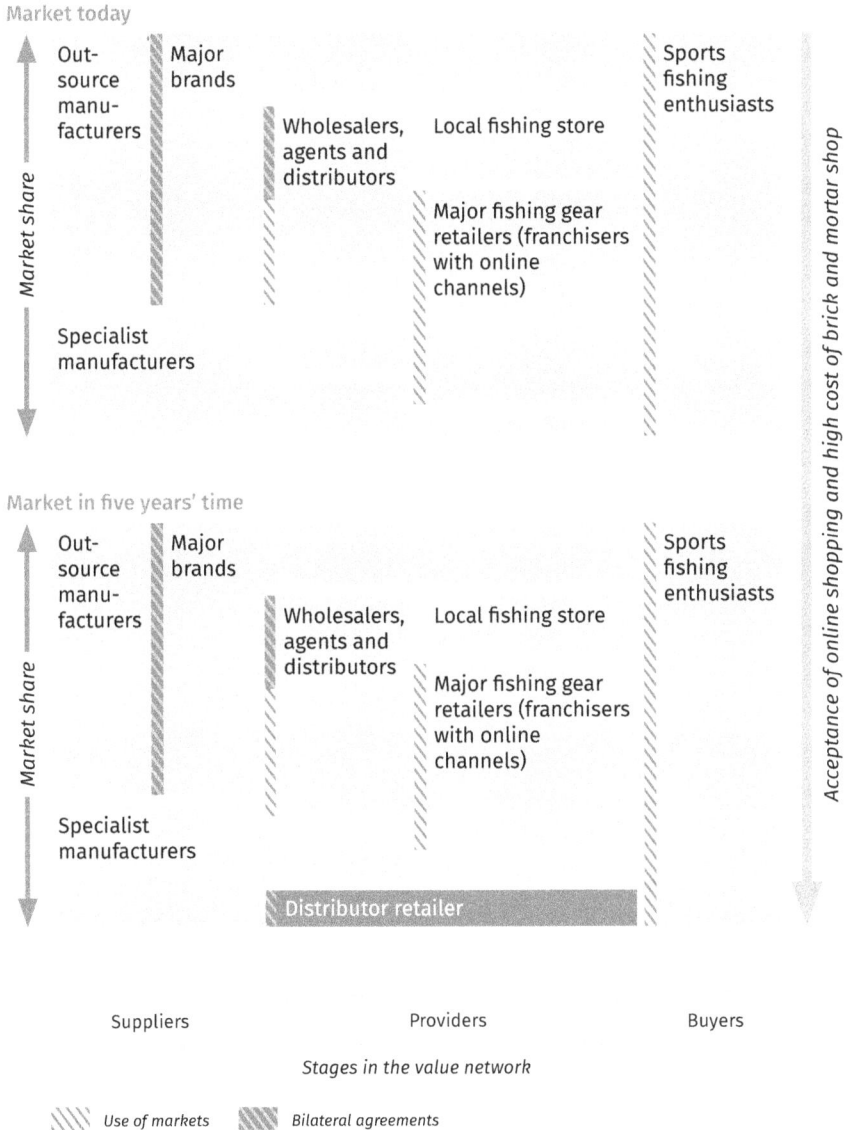

Market today

Market share ↑↓

Out-source manu-facturers

Major brands

Wholesalers, agents and distributors

Local fishing store

Major fishing gear retailers (franchisers with online channels)

Sports fishing enthusiasts

Specialist manufacturers

Acceptance of online shopping and high cost of brick and mortar shop

Market in five years' time

Market share ↑↓

Out-source manu-facturers

Major brands

Wholesalers, agents and distributors

Local fishing store

Major fishing gear retailers (franchisers with online channels)

Sports fishing enthusiasts

Specialist manufacturers

Distributor retailer

Suppliers

Providers

Buyers

Stages in the value network

▨ *Use of markets*   ▨ *Bilateral agreements*

3

3.2
Market sizing

Overview

The value map requires estimates of the market share of each of the key players or group of players (buyers, competitors and suppliers). These estimates are the first step in: identifying the buyers, sizing the revenue opportunity, sourcing key inputs, understanding the nature of the contractual relationships used by buyers and suppliers, and the challenge from alternatives or complements.

Method

This is an exploratory exercise and a range of different techniques are used to gain this information. For people already well versed in the industry they may know most of this information and this exercise is to document that knowledge. For opportunities involving new ventures this exercise focuses on identifying likely buyers/suppliers/related products or groups of these.

In many situations, for example for most small businesses providing a well-recognised product it may appear that buyers are plentiful and simple sales contracts are used– and therefore a large easily accessible market exists. If there are many competing providers of the product, and buyers can easily find alternative providers then the market share that the business can address may be small. The number of potential buyers that can be reached has several considerations such as geographic, jurisdiction, ability to market to those potential buyers, and their readiness to buy. These latter considerations can dominate business-to-business sales and the launch of a new product to the market. Here more complex contractual relationships may be used. With products with limited number of buyers, pre-orders may be the best gauge of market size. These same considerations apply to input suppliers.

The coverage of this enquiry is:

1. Target buyers:

   › Who are the key or type of target buyers?

   › What is the size of each segment?

   › What is the growth profile of each segment?

2. Key competitors and what is known about them:

   › Who are the key or types of competitors?

   › What is the market share/ revenue of each type of competitor?

3. Key suppliers:

   › Who are the key or types of suppliers?

   › What is the market share of each type of supplier?

4. Related products:

   › Does the product have substitutable or complementary products?

   › What is the nature of the relationship and contractual relationships being used?

   › What is the market size of these related products?

3

3.3
Trends & their impact

Overview

The value network map depicts the key players that make up the value network and their relative market share. The value network map also identifies the nature of the contractual relationships used by businesses. It is used to show the location of the business opportunity in relation to all the relevant players in the value network and the impact of macro trends in shaping the value network.

Method

To depict the impact of money flows over time a value network map would be compiled for each point in time so that the changes can be compared. One of the uses of the value network map is to establish who controls the allocation of value added in the value network.

The analysis then seeks to draw conclusions about:

What gaps can be anticipated in the value network because of the macro trends?

› What is the relationship of gaps to the opportunity and how might the gaps be expected to be filled?

› What is the impact of macro trends on the urgency in exploiting the opportunity and its lifespan?

› What changes in market trajectory and future shape of the value network can be anticipated from success of the venture?

A process to develop a value network map is:

› *Step 1 –* Map the key players in the value network by place in the value network and market share. The value network should capture at least three stages in the value network, the buyers, competitors and suppliers of the business that will be applying the opportunity. Note that the scope in relation to the specific area of business will dictate what is perceived as the value network. This is *Section 3.1: The value network.*

› *Step 2 –* Identify the macro trends in change in the structure of the value network. This can be done by depicting, using market share, at each stage in the value network, the situation today, that five years ago and the situation expected in five years time. This analysis should note any changes in players, products and market share. The emphasis here is to track the impact of the flow of money over time. This is important because the business opportunity will be trying to find ways to share in this flow of money.

› *Step 3 –* Establish points where high transaction cost exist, and the nature of the contractual relationships used in the market.

› For market disrupting products, *Step 4* is to depict the structure of the value network in five years time were the venture is successful. For many ventures, their success does not noticeably change the structure of the value network, and their focus would be to find a cluster of businesses they can join with, to share in the available value added.

Considerations in placing the opportunity in the value network and macro trends are:

1. Place the opportunity in the value network of the relevant element markets:

   › Who are the major players or categories of players covering buyers, competitors and suppliers, substitutes and complements related to the opportunity (from *Section 3.1: The value network*)?

   › Are there other parties relevant to the description of the opportunity in the value network because they share in the available value added (such as key resource owners)?

   › What are their relative market shares and growth rate?

   › What are the market coordination mechanisms between stages in the value network and are there any special coordination mechanisms?

2. Market context is used to identify the important macro trends:

   › What macro factors (social structure and demographic,

business, economic, technological, government and environmental) are important in characterising the market context of the value network?

› Does the impact of these factors differ in different parts of the value network?

3. Macro trends which will change the shape of the value network, and therefore impact on the business opportunity:

› What macro trends are at play across the value network that have been evident in changing its shape over the last five years?

› What has been the impact of macro trends on the shared transaction costs?

› What are the forecast macro trends and the expected impact on the value network over the next five years?

› What is the forecast impact of macro trends on the shared transaction costs?

The idea behind transaction costs is to place buying decisions within a process that starts with the search costs of finding the product and information to make decisions about products, and then all subsequent steps through to culmination in the decision to buy and then its use. The transaction cost is a measure of the difficulty the buyer faces in making the first best decision (discussed in more detail in *Section 4.2: Customer journey*).

An example of a value network map is given in *Figure 9*.

BUYERS & THE FRICTION THEY FACE

4.1
Target buyers

Overview

Unlike the description of the value network which takes a high-level view of the market, this section considers who are the target buyers, and the perceived benefits being sought in the product. This enquiry sets out to understand: the identity of buyers and their wants; pricing expectations and budget constraints; the transaction cost in buying and using the product; and the market feedback effects that might operate on buyers.

The target market is a subset of the market in *Section 3.2: Market sizing* where the total market size that the project could access was estimated. Target buyers are the buyers that will provide the target revenue over the planning period.

Method

The consumer of a product may not be synonymous with the buyer, for example, the buyer of after-school tuition for students, and aged-care services may respectively be parents, and children. It is the wants of the decision maker that need to be described. The decision-making criteria also change from one setting to another. For example, public sector decision makers must demonstrate adherence to due process, may select health care products within the approved budget, based on: (1) patient outcome; (2) risk of things going wrong; and (3) price. These criteria may be quite different to those used by an individual when purchasing health care products.

Buyer wants are perceived benefits for which buyers will want more of it, and are very different to those benefits that they will actually pay for. In a market setting the issue is to understand these perceived benefits, whether they are: functional attributes of the product, motivations of buyers, aspirations of buyers, product meaning e.g. brand association, or availability expectations e.g. channel and place.

Also influencing buyers' decisions are market feedback effects. For example, a product may be associated with belonging to a particular social group (bandwagon effect), or maybe it is fashionable or subject to strong word-of-mouth referrals (both social network effects). These market feedback effects can work positively to enhance demand for a product, as well as negatively to dampen demand.

The scope of buyer considerations is:

1. Identity of target buyers:

   › Who are the target buyers e.g. the consumer and/or decision maker?

   › How are they distinguishable?

2. Buyer wants covering, what are the:

   › functional attributes;

   › motivations of buyers;

   › aspirations of buyers;

   › product meaning e.g. brand association; and

   › availability expectations e.g. channel and place?

3. Monetary considerations:

   › What are the price expectations; and

   › the budget constraints?

4. Market feedback effects:

   › Are their bandwagon; and/or

   › social network effects at play?

4

4.2
Customer journey

Overview

Having described buyers and their needs, this immediately raises questions about the customer journey from their initial identification and search for information through the buying decision, to on-boarding and after sales service. Of interest during this journey are the sources of the friction experience by the buyer, how significant is it, and what can be done about improving the perceived benefit to the customer?

Understanding the nature of the friction buyers face is important as it determines competitive strategies, activity types available, nature of contracts that are used as part of the product offer.

Some transaction costs are important sources of business opportunities – such as those associated with information asymmetries. For example, professional services and retailing businesses are based on the existence of information asymmetries. The focus of this section is on the transaction costs faced by the customer when buying and consuming a product.

Method

Businesses and consumers incur costs when transacting with one another, these are referred to as transaction costs. Some examples of the transaction costs faced in buying and using a product are:

› Difficulty in finding the product and supplier.

› Cost of having to settle for the second-best alternative.

› Cost of selecting, negotiating and paying for the product.

› Barriers to access or consume the product.

› Cost of being left with a 'lemon' and avoiding bad lemons.

› Consequences of the transaction failing and having to rectify the situation.

Figure 7 shows a customer journey map that focuses on the friction buyers face in having their expectations met. The customer journey is made up of two elements: the first is the process that the buyers face in engaging with the product; and in parallel to this, the buyer's experience in engaging in the process. A key factor determining this experience is the expectation of the buyer which is shaped by prior experience, and claims made by the provider and competitors. The customer journey map shows these two elements as well as identified improvements to the product attributes.

The customer journey makes a distinction between high level stages,

the processes that the buyer is involved in in each stage, and product attributes that align to the process. Buyers' views are related to processes. The gap between experience and expectation is friction encountered by the buyer and/or deficiencies in other aspects of the product offering, and this gives clues on the points of difference to be accentuated in the product benefits. Frequently, changes in product offering have financial implications and refining the product offering is a costly, iterative process.

Considerations in preparing a high-level customer journey map to identify the transaction costs faced in buying and using the product are:

› The product and target buyers.

› Ease of finding the product.

› Significance of lemons.

› Ease of transacting

› Ease of accessing/consuming.

› Steps to avoid consequences of provider failure.

› Ease of onboarding.

› After sales support.

Also relevant in considering the buyer's decision-making process are the impacts of market feedback effects such as: the bandwagon effect, and social network effects.

While a simple retail operation is shown in the diagram, a range of different conditions can arise that will determine the nature of the contractual arrangement put in place. This is particularly the case for business-to-business sales. The contract types available are outlined in *Section 7.1: Contractual relationships* which by extension also apply to the buyer relationship.

Figure 10 Illustrative customer journey map

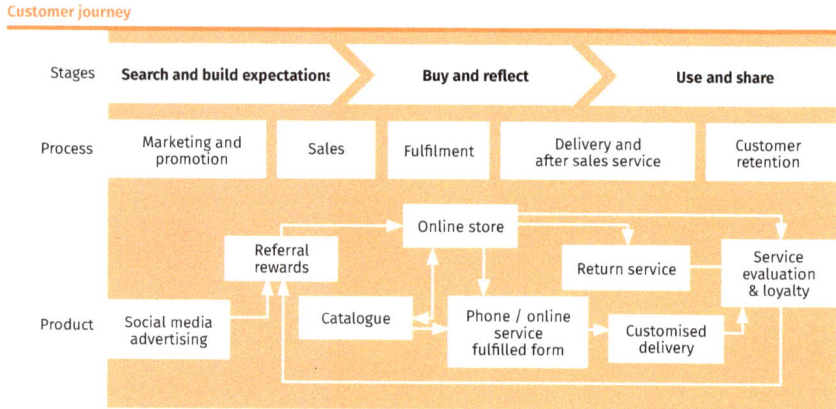

Customer journey

Stages	**Search and build expectations**		**Buy and reflect**		**Use and share**
Process	Marketing and promotion	Sales	Fulfilment	Delivery and after sales service	Customer retention

Product:
- Social media advertising
- Referral rewards
- Catalogue
- Online store
- Phone / online service fulfilled form
- Return service
- Customised delivery
- Service evaluation & loyalty

Buyer experience

Buyer expectation	"I want to shop where the pros shop"	"I want something that works"	"I want it now"	"I want to feel I am a valued customer"
Buyer experience		"Difficult to find what I want"	"Don't have what I want in stock"	"I wish I could change it"
Friction encountered	"I can't find locally made products"	"Can I trust this store?"		

Product offering

Points of difference	Information from pros on species and location	Products from specialist manufacturers	Delivery service standards	Reviews and tips from pros
Benefits	Wide range of products from specialist manufacturers	Reliable product information and use tips	Competitively priced quality products	"We value our customers"

4

4.3
Product attributes

Overview

The bundle of attributes put forward in the product and its service delivery are presented to the buyer as a value proposition, explaining how the offer matches buyers' needs for the price, given budget constraints, and how it is the best value-for-money compared to all other competing offers. The experience of a product's value-for-money to stakeholders so that it results in a decision to act is the value proposition.

The purpose of this enquiry is to describe the perceived benefits that the product holds for the buyer. Products are the device to share in the available value added. This enquiry sets out to understand:

1. the alignment between the perceived value-for-money of the product and buyers' needs

2. the effectiveness of the proposed communications of the product's value-for-money to buyers; and

3. the resultant effectiveness of the sales and service.

The components of the offer, satisfying buyers' needs, are put forward as a value proposition, explaining how the offer matches buyers' needs for the price, given budget constraints, and how it is the best value-for-money compared to all other competing offers.

Method

There are three components to the process of offering a product for sale, and its conversion into an actual sale:

1. The components of the product offering making up the value proposition:

   › What category type is the product?

   › What are the product attributes?

   › What are the attributes of the service process (including the ceremony, place and people)?

   › What price is to apply?

   › What distribution channels are to be used?

   › Where is the product to be positioned in the market?

   › What meaning is attached to the product by buyers?

2. The communication of the product offering and its interpretation by buyers and conversion into the action to buy:

   › What is the message encapsulating the value proposition?

   › Which media channels are to be used to reach the target buyers?

   › Who will be the receivers of this message and how are they related to the buying decision maker?

   › How is the received message interpreted in meeting needs and the veracity of the message when compared to alternatives?

   › What is the buying decision-making process?

   › How effective is the communications i.e. how easy is it for the buyer to find the product?

3. The sales and service component:

   › What degree of asset specificity is involved in the product for the provider?

   › What contract type is being used and how does it compare to the contracts used by competitors (see *Section 7.1: Contractual relationships*)?

   › Where applicable, what is the on-boarding process?

> How easy is it to buy and use the product?

For a new to market product, this analysis should be undertaken for the minimum viable product that can be taken to market to test the proposition.

DEMAND, ALTERNATIVES & COMPETITION

5

5.1
Competing products

Overview

The purpose of this exercise is to establish the alternatives the target buyers (identified in *Section 4.1: Target buyers*) can choose from, and the level of demand for each alternative observed in the market.

Competitors offer a range of products at different price/benefit combinations. *Figure 11A* depicts a market supplied by products (A & B) with different perceived benefits. The third supplier provides a high benefit product at a correspondingly higher price. The two products nonetheless provide the same value-for-money to buyers, the constant value-for-money curve shows that relationship. In a market with well-informed buyers, no supplier providing poorer value-for-money would make sales (such a product would be depicted above the constant value-for-money curve). The relationship between price and sales is described in demand curves. The demand curve shows the price/quantity relationship for a product of constant benefit. The demand curve for higher benefit products is shifted to the right of the lower benefit product. While the illustration in *Figure 11A* shows two demand curves, at this point in the analysis the only thing known about the shape of the demand curve is the point estimate of observed prices and sales. The sales of the product A are split between the providers – the split is their respective market share.

For new products with no competitors, a market testing process is undertaken to identify from where spending is to be diverted in favour of the new product. For digital products a 'minimum viable product' would be built to demonstrate the planned product attributes.

Figure 11 Value-for-money indifference and demand curves

A *Market with two competing products, A and B*

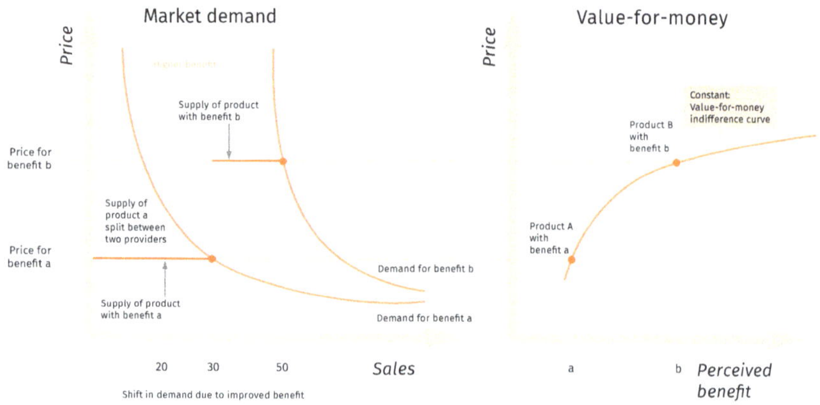

Market demand

Price

Supply of product with benefit b

Price for benefit b

Supply of product a split between two providers

Price for benefit a

Supply of product with benefit a

Demand for benefit b

Demand for benefit a

20   30   50   Sales

Shift in demand due to improved benefit

Value-for-money

Price

Constant: Value-for-money indifference curve

Product B with benefit b

Product A with benefit a

a   b   Perceived benefit

B *Perceived market opportunity to offer product C (taking market share from product B)*

Market demand

Price

Price for benefit b

Target price

Price for benefit a

Demand for benefit b

Demand for benefit a

20   30   50   Sales

40   Target sales

Value-for-money

Price

Constant: Value-for-money indifference curve

Product B with benefit b

Planned market position for new product C

Product A with benefit a

a   b   Perceived benefit

c

C *Provider of product B responds by increasing its value-for-money (potentially cornering the entire market)*

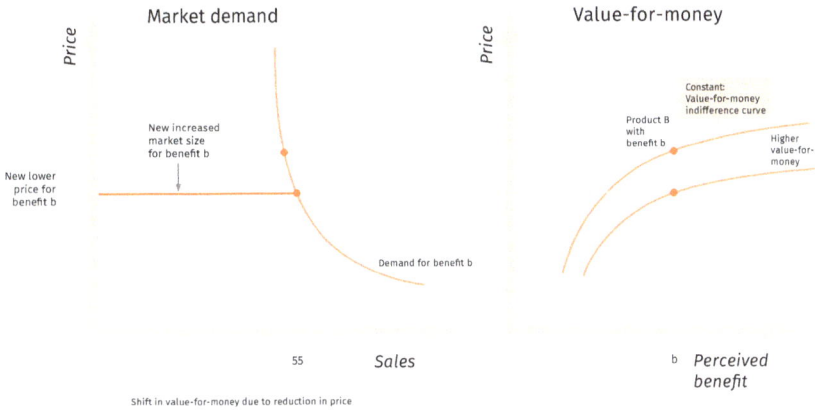

Market demand

Price

New increased
market size
for benefit b

New lower
price for
benefit b

Demand for benefit b

55   *Sales*

Shift in value-for-money due to reduction in price

Value-for-money

Price

Constant:
Value-for-money
indifference curve

Product B
with
benefit b

Higher
value-for-
money

b   *Perceived
benefit*

Method

The value proposition and the market demand curves provide insight into the relative position of the product in the market and demand. The data used to compile this is drawn from market research, and covers:

> the alternative products;

> their perceived benefits to buyers;

> price; and

> sales volumes.

Considerations in establishing the alternatives buyers face in the market for the proposed product are:

1. Value proposition and sharing in the available value added:

   > What are the perceived benefits valued by buyers based on meeting their needs?

   > What are the benefits and price of the product supplied by each provider?

   > How has value-for-money of the competing products changed over the last five years?

   > How is value-for-money of the competing products expected to change over the next five years?

2. Gaining a share of value added:

   > In what ways could the market be disrupted by changing products and their value-for-money?

   > How easy would it be to find competing products?

   > Have ways to circumvent the value controller been identified?

A value controller has high bargaining power that is used to exert control over the allocation of value added in a value network. One form of value controller is a multisided platform operator. Suppliers into these platforms are complements to the platform and their future is tied to the success of the platform.

5

5.2
Target revenue

Overview

Demand and value proposition curves depict the size of the market and the position in the market of the key players. One of the key outputs from this analysis is an estimate of the target revenue, and equally important how this revenue is to be realised. Where there is no existing market for the product, knowledge on how to drive sales will need to be acquired.

The failure of many new ventures can be attributed to insufficient attention being given to understanding buyers, and the marketing and sales process to those buyers. The exercise of estimating the potential revenue must be undertaken simultaneously with an explanation of how these revenues are to be realised. Rigorous market validation of the product value proposition and revenue estimates would be undertaken in subsequent stages in the business planning process. Even the best ideas can fail without an appropriate go-to-market approach and resourcing.

The outputs of this enquiry are:

› Description of the ideal customer profile that are thought to be suited to the idea.

› Estimate of the target addressable market size for the idea.

The process to estimate the target addressable market is illustrated in *Figure 11B*. Here a new product C with perceived benefits of C is to be offered at a target price to place the product on the constant value-for-money curve. At the target price 10 units of sales can be expected. In this simple example, these sales are taken from the sales of product B.

Method

Considerations in how these outputs are to be developed are:

1. Buyers being targeted:

   › The profile of the ideal buyer and their number; and

   › Number of buyers.

2. Assumptions about buyers. Assumptions impact the size of the addressable market and market share, and need to be translated into actions to be performed by the venture's sales capabilities. Those aspects are discussed below. Having taken these considerations and the competitor product benefit/price/demand into account, the estimate of the targeted revenue is dependent on:

   › price to be charged;

   › buyers to be targeted;

   › effectiveness of actions to make sales;

   › understanding of the key factors in successfully making sales; and

   › critical assumptions being made about the revenue target.

5

5.3
Competitive threats

Overview

In the context of the planned market positioning and target revenue, the purpose of this section is to lay out potential threats posed by competitors to realising those plans.

Method

The most common situation in highly competitive markets is of competitors continuously improving the value-for-money of their products. The effect of this is to shift the constant value-for-money curve to the right – as shown in *Figure 11C.* In the example of a new perceived opportunity being to new product C, then the competitive response of the provider of the higher benefit product B could be to reduce the price of B, and in doing so provide higher value-for-money than A or C. This effectively destroys their value propositions. The value proposition and demand curves can be used to analyse the impact of likely competitive responses.

There are five market positioning strategies available:

> **Position 1** Cost advantage where the business has a lower average cost structure, compared to competitors, achieved through choice of activity type and place in the value network, and having the ability to supply products at a lower unit price for equivalent benefits than competitors.

> **Position 2** Local advantage where the lower cost to a supplier of reaching local buyers is exploited.

> **Position 3** Extemporaneous advantage stemming from conditions where buyers are willing to pay a premium because of a product's availability at the right time and place.

> **Position 4** Segmentation advantage where the attributes of the product are changed to provide a targeted sub-group of buyers with better value-for-money than competing products.

In response to reductions in transaction cost, both high value-for-money advantage and cost advantage are robust responses. Whereas, a general reduction in transaction cost undermines extemporaneous, local and transaction cost advantages.

Considerations in assessing competitive threats are:

> What market positioning strategies have been adopted by the various players?

> Whether transaction costs can be removed?

> Which of the competitors has cost advantage over the others?

> Is there a window of time where demand exceeds supply?

> Can the market be segmented?

These considerations are discussed in *Facet 4: Buyers and the friction they face.*

PRO-
DUCTION
PROCESS

6

6.1
Choosing an activity type

Overview

The key step in creating a business angle is the matching of an activity type to the perceived opportunity to realise the aims within the constraints of the venture. This section discusses the selection of an activity type, and therefore creating a business angle.

In selecting an activity type, the question being explored is: What are the business angles which could be used to insert a proposed business venture into a value network? The question is answered using the activity type matrix to consider for each of the methods of delivery and for acquiring inputs how they could be applied in the value network to create a business angle for the perceived business opportunity. A significant challenge in this, is to be able to imagine activity types which in the market context being looked at may not exist. This requires in addition to a clear understanding of the market opportunity, a detailed understanding of buyers and other participants in the value network. Familiarity with an activity type makes it easy to envisage its application to the perceived opportunity, but makes it more challenging to consider the place of alternatives.

Method

The activity type matrix provides a tool for describing the range of quite different activity types available to pursue a business opportunity based on the processes used to deliver outputs and acquire inputs. Four generic methods are used for acquiring inputs and four for delivering outputs giving 16 distinct activity types. A method requires knowhow, systems, processes and procedures to be put in place and these are designed to meet the specific requirements of the business angle. The **assemble method** is concerned with transition products, the **assign method** with outsourcing for capacity, the **aggregate method** with realising network and pooling effects, and **arbitrage** with exploiting imperfections in the market.

The purpose is to identify business angles with no concern at this point as to it's feasibility or viability. In undertaking this analysis, several activity types are likely to be identified which are not currently offered in the market because they are neither feasible nor viable.

The taxonomy of activity types is given in *Figure 12.* The most recognisable activity type is the *'Producer' (a: assemble-assemble)* in which the business uses own resources for the delivery of output and its own resources to acquire inputs. Having started with this commonly found activity type, it can be easy to work down the column considering the differing methods of acquiring inputs keeping the delivery method constant, for example if starting with activity type **a,** to then consider activity types **e** *(Systems Integrator),* i *(Supplier Cooperative)* and m *(Assembler).*

The aggregate method of delivering outputs can be the next most commonly recognised and the activity types **c** *(Network Operator),* **g** *(Consolidator),* k *(Insurer)* and o *(Aggregator)* completed successively.

Also easily recognised, is the arbitrage-arbitrage activity type (p), which may be easier to complete the arbitrage column by considering activity types in the following order: **p** *(Trader),* l *(Auctioneer),* h *(Agent)* and d *(Developer).*

The assign method of delivering outputs can be the most problematic to identify examples of as this method relies on economies from networks and large numbers and drawing on illustrations from the insurance and finance sectors is useful here. For the assign method the suggested order of completing the column is **b** *(Outsource Provider),* f *(Lead Contractor),* j *(Underwriter)* and n *(Broker).*

Figure 12 Taxonomy of activity types

Delivery method

Acquisition method	(Assemble)	(Assign)	(Aggregate)	(Arbitrage)
(Assemble)	**a. Producer** Production of products by using inputs that require significant processing	**b. Outsource supplier** Supply of capacity based on utilising inputs that require significant pre-processing	**c. Network operator** Construction of a portfolio of purchasers of products that utilise inputs requiring significant transformation	**d. Developer** Resale of products derived from inputs requiring significant preparation
(Assign)	**e. Systems integrator** Production of products utilising contracted operational capacity from third parties	**f. Lead contractor** Supply of capacity by utilising contracted operational capacity from third parties	**g. Consolidator** Construction of a portfolio of purchasers of products supplied from operational capacity contracted from third parties	**h. Agent** Resale of contracted operational capacity from third parties
(Aggregate)	**i. Supplier cooperative** Production of products by engaging with a portfolio of input suppliers	**j. Underwriter** Supply of capacity by using capacity syndicated to several suppliers	**k. Insurer** Construction of a portfolio of purchasers of products that is syndicated to a portfolio of suppliers	**l. Auctioneer** Resale of products acquired from a range of input suppliers
(Arbitrage)	**m. Assembler** Production of products based on bought in sub-assembly componentry	**n. Broker** Supply of capacity by on-selling capacity from suppliers	**o. Aggregator** Construction of a portfolio of purchasers for products acquired for reselling	**p. Trader** Trading in products

Figure 13 provides a way to locate a starting activity type from which to then explore other activity types that can then be used to identify a candidate business angle. The range of activity types that correspond to the selected delivery and acquisition methods are elaborated in *Section 6.2: Supporting capabilities.*

Figure 13 Questions to establish the candidate delivery and acquisition methods

	The prime source of economies being exploited in:	Delivery method
Delivering outputs	Does this product make it easier to get other products?	■● ▲✗
	Are you buying a product which depends on the law of large numbers?	✦
	Does this product provide capacity or access to a network?	✦
	Is this a new product distinguishable from its component parts?	⊕

		Acquisition method
Acquiring inputs	Are these the products which are on-sold?	■● ▲✗
	Is risk being passed to another party?	✦
	Is capacity contracted for?	✦
	Are input components bought or hired?	⊕

Considerations in selecting the activity type are:

1. Alternative activity types and corresponding business angles:

   › What degree of speculation is to be undertaken?

   › What resources are available to the venture?

   › What activity type is most appropriate for the aim and resourcing?

   › Do these activity types create a business angle to exploit the opportunity?

2. Capability and their alignment to the market:

   › What capabilities are required to deliver the business angle?

   › What capabilities can be used to create core competencies?

3. Creation of core competencies:

   › Are any existing core competencies or other scarce resources being exploited?

   › Which declining cost economies are to be exploited to create core competencies?

4. Supporting organisational structure:

   › What organisational architecture is to be used to coordinate the capabilities?

6

6.2
Supporting capabilities

Overview

Activity types consist of output delivery and input acquisition methods. The methods are given effect through capabilities. These capabilities and their information flows give rise to core competencies, which consume inputs, to generate profits. The purpose of this section is to identify the essential capabilities and the associated information flows and causes of cash flow.

Method

The selection of an activity type determines the capabilities used to exploit the perceived opportunity. As an illustration, some capabilities of a retail enterprise utilising the arbitrage-arbitrage activity type are depicted in *Figure 14.* Most capabilities support a single method, but there are some capabilities participating in both delivery and acquisition methods – in the diagram, the finance and compliance capability is an example of this. Each capability performs a bundle of functions. The scope of the functions is determined by the complexity of the business.

The capabilities and information flow diagram also shows the key information flows between capabilities. The information flows highlight only the key dependency relationships. The information flows show the information and communications systems that are essential to the coordination of the capabilities.

In addition to information flows, there are cash flows associated with each capability. Knowhow, systems and processes of the capabilities consume and generate these cash flows – for example, from the purchase and sale of products. A capability, input/ output diagram is used to record the key information and causes of cash flow by a capability. *Figure 15* shows the capability, input/ output diagram for the example shown in *Figure 14*.

Figure 14 Capabilities and information flow diagram of a retail venture utilising the arbitrage-arbitrage activity type

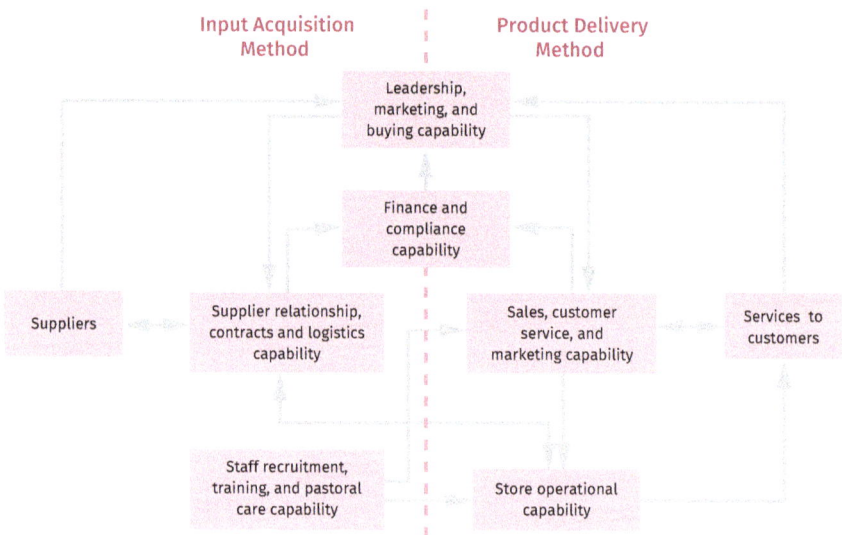

Figure 15 High-level capability, input/output diagram for retail venture

Inputs	Capabilities	Outputs
Key people with ability to interpret market trends Sales and customer performance measures Financial performance measures	Leadership, strategy and buying	Buying directions
Financial commitments Cash receipts	Finance and compliance	Financial commitments Cash payments Financial performance measures Compliance information
Suppliers	Supplier relationship, contracts and logistics	Purchase orders Supplier relationships Financial commitments Fulfilment of customer orders
Applicants Staff	Staff recruitment, training and pastoral care	Suitable staff with high morale
Suitable sales and customer service staff Customer feedback Cash from sales	Sales, customer service and marketing	Sales Sales and customer performance measures
Premises Stock People experienced in UX design	Store operations	Ecommerce store Fulfilment of customer orders

6

6.3
Knowhow, systems & processes

Overview

This enquiry sets out to describe at a high level the knowhow, systems and processes to provide the required functionality of the identified capabilities. Consistent with the activity type being used, this enquiry also identifies their sources, which can be:

› Purchased from outside suppliers (discussed further in *Section 7.1: Contractual relationships* and *Section 7.2: Cost of systems & processes*).

› Core business operations (*Section 7.3: Costs of operating*).

› Built (see *Section 8.3: Capacity initiatives*).

› Knowhow provided by key people (*Section 6.4: Leadership & key people*).

Method

There are two elements to the high-level design of the systems and processes required to give effect to the capabilities that make up the activity type:

› the knowhow, systems and processes underpinning the capability; and

› the information and communications systems to enable capabilities or parties (buyers, suppliers etc.) to work together.

Considerations in identifying the knowhow, systems and processes are:

› For each capability, what systems and processes are required to underpin the functionality?

› For each information flow, what are the information and communications systems required to provide the needed coordination?

› What knowhow is required to operate the systems and processes?

› Are other capacities required?

› Where is the knowhow, systems and processes, and other capacity to be obtained, and does any require building?

› What is the implication of these sourcing of the knowhow, systems and processes, and other capacity on cash flows?

› Are any of the information flows associated with cash flows?

An example of a high-level identification of the costs for systems and processes is given in *Figure 16.* In this example:

› Systems and processes implemented include finance and enterprise resource planning (ERP), point of sale (POS) and online store. In these three cases the systems and processes are to be provided by outside suppliers.

› Industry knowledge is required for the buying function to curate a suitable line of merchandise. This knowledge requires on-going involvement in the market through engagement with influential buyers, suppliers and other stakeholders.

› New knowhow must be created in online sales.

Figure 16 High-level systems and processes, and requisite knowhow and other capacity to provide the requisite functionality

	Parties		Information management system
Initiator capability	Counterparty	Information flow	
Leadership, strategy and buying	Suppliers	Supplier arrangements	Email/phone
	Supplier relationship, and contracts	Negotiated arrangements	Finance and ERP
	Customers	Market trends, performance in market, opportunities	Email/phone
	Sales, customer service and marketing	Strategic directions	Finance and ERP, Collaboration
Finance and compliance	Leadership, strategy and buying	Performance assessments	Finance and ERP
Supplier relationship, contracts, and logistics	Suppliers	Customer orders, stock levels, logistics performance	Email/phone, Fulfilment
	Store operations	Stock levels, delivery performance	Finance and ERP
Staff recruitment, training and pastoral care	Sales, customer service and marketing / Store operations	Training and pastoral care	Training, Collaboration
Sales, customer service and marketing	Store operations	Product information, pricing, promotions	Online store, digital marketing tools
	Finance and compliance	Sales targets, market performance	Finance and ERP
	Customer	Digital marketing, customer experience	Email/phone, CRM
Store operations	Customers	Information on products, purchasing terms and conditions, shopping basket, payment collection, performance feedback	Online store, Fulfilment system, POS system

A description of the information and communications systems for the key information flows identified in *Figure 14* is given in *Figure 17*. Other than email and phone, key information systems are:

> Finance and ERP system,

> POS system; and

> Online store.

These three systems are identified as key systems required to provide functionality of various capabilities, and are identified in *Figure 16* – in this example the description of the information and communications systems in *Figure 14*. *Figure 17* serves as a cross check that the key systems and processes have been identified.

The analysis of the knowhow, systems and processes, and associated information flows, is placed in context of specifying their source and implications on cash flows. The sources are determined by the business angle design. These sources, and some of the information flows, have implications for cash flows.

Figure 17 High-level information and communications systems to support key information flows

Capabilities	Knowhow capable of creating core competencies	Systems and process	Other capacity
Leadership, strategy and buying	Industry knowledge and contacts to put in place supply agreements Industry knowledge of trends in customer preferences	Email/ phone CRM Fulfilment Finance and ERP Collaboration Online store	Premise Office workstations and equipment
Finance and compliance	Operation of capability	Digital marketing tools	
Supplier relationship, contracts, and logistics	Operation of capability	POS system Training	
Staff recruitment, training and pastoral care	Operation of capability		
Sales, customer service and marketing	New knowhow must be created in online marketing and sales making to target market segment		
Store operations	Operation of capability		

Appraising Business Opportunities

6.4
Leadership & key people

Overview

A key consideration in the evaluation of a venture is the skill and experience of the key people involved. The aim of this investigation is to explain the skill and experience available, and its relevance. How these skills and experience contribute to the success of the venture are elaborated in *Facet 8: Initiatives for a successful outcome.*

Method

Considerations in evidencing the leadership and knowhow available to the project are:

1. For each of the areas in which knowhow is important (identified in *Section 6.3: Knowhow, systems & processes,* and *Section 8.1: Success & assumptions*):

   › What matters is the knowhow to address?

   › How is the knowhow to be obtained?

   › What is the price of accessing this knowhow?

FACET 6: Production process

65

- › How is the persons on-going contribution to be secured?

- › What is the cost to severing the arrangements?

- › What alternative sources of the knowhow are available?

- › What is the price of the alternative?

2. For each of the key people involved in the project:

   - › What are their relevant skills and experience?How will they be recruited?

   - › How will they be retained?

   - › What is to be their role in the project?

   - › How will their skill and experience be contributed?

   - › What will they do to make a difference?

   - › What are the key performance indicators to show that they are making a difference?

Appraising Business Opportunities

SUPPLIERS & PART-NERS

7.1

Contractual relationships

Overview

The question answered in this facet of compiling a scoping business plan is: how much will it cost to operate a venture using the production process described in *Facet 6: Production process*? At one level, dealing with suppliers and partners is simply the cost of acquiring inputs. At another level, acquiring inputs is one of the five contributors of FCF value to the business (Contributor 2).

The costs (cash outflows) of a venture are categorised into those related to:

› acquiring the various capabilities and their underpinning knowhow, systems and processes; and

› operating the production process to deliver planned outputs, for example using purchased inputs.

These categories of cost are discussed in the next two sections. The remainder of this section discusses the different contractual arrangements that buyers and suppliers enter, and are the market coordination mechanisms identified in the analysis of the value network (*Section 3.1: The value network*). There is another category of cost, associated with the specific initiatives to bring about change, and these are discussed in *Facet 8: Initiatives for a successful outcome.*

Businesses use a range of different contractual relationships when working with one another. The most appropriate arrangement is the one providing the most economical acquisition of inputs to support a highly productive production process. *Figure 18* provides a decision tree showing the different conditions leading to different purchasing practices, risk sharing, contract type, quality assurance mechanisms, asset ownership and control, and governance arrangements.

Key questions

Some of the factors that influence the costs and risks of contracting are whether:

Q1. The input can be clearly defined and specified at the outset?

Q2. There is a competitive market of suppliers?

Q3. Prospective suppliers are prepared to make the investment required to deliver the product?

Q4. The risk adjusted cost of failure to the buyer is high?

Q5. Poor performance is easily identifiable and can be monitored, and risk mitigated at a suitable price?

These factors are considered in selecting the appropriate form of contractual relationships with suppliers of each input, as discussed in the following sections. The same considerations are used to establish the appropriate contractual relationship for a venture's products with its customers (discussed in *Section 4.2: Customer journey*).

Figure 18 Decision tree of some factors influencing the selection of a contractual relationship for acquiring inputs

The product to which the contractual relationship is to be applied

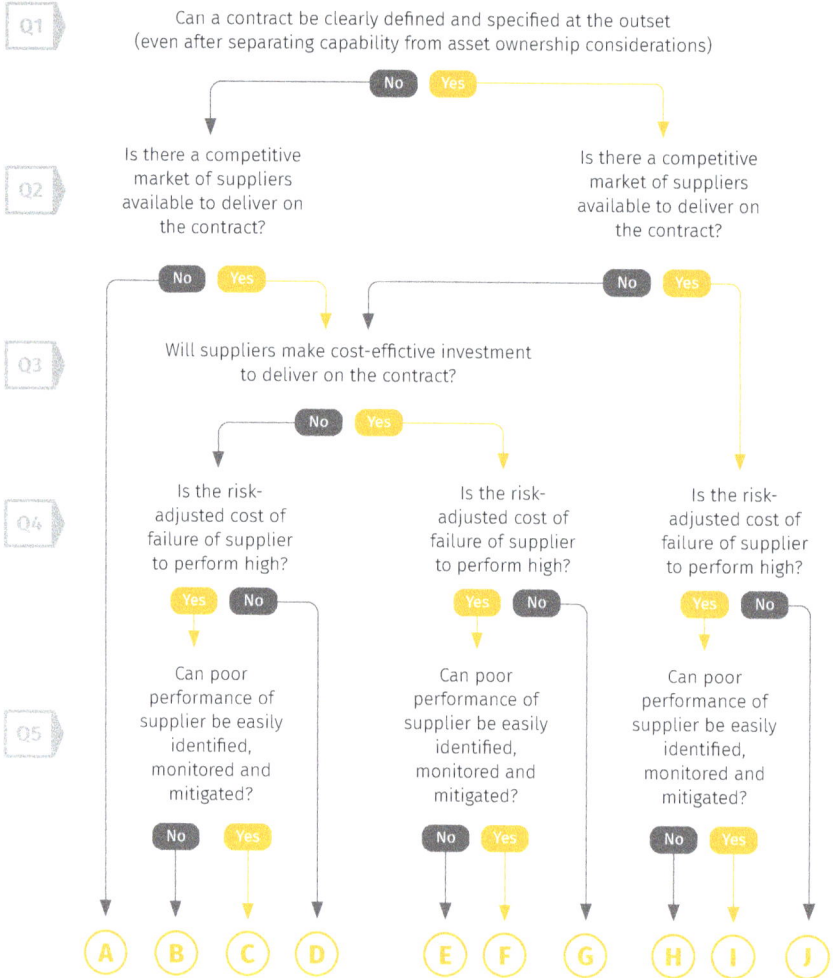

Q1 — Can a contract be clearly defined and specified at the outset (even after separating capability from asset ownership considerations)

No / Yes

Q2 — Is there a competitive market of suppliers available to deliver on the contract?

No / Yes

Q3 — Will suppliers make cost-effictive investment to deliver on the contract?

No / Yes

Q4 — Is the risk-adjusted cost of failure of supplier to perform high?

Yes / No

Q5 — Can poor performance of supplier be easily identified, monitored and mitigated?

No / Yes

A B C D   E F G   H I J

Figure 18 cont'd

	A	B	C	D	E	F	G	H	I	J
Form of product	Capability & capacity			Capability			Capacity			Mainly complete
Procurement practice	Manage in-house		Preferred supplier		Competitive tender where price/quality are traded off					Selected on weighted attributes
Contractual relationship	Unified	▓			Bilateral					Market
Special quality assurance mechanisms										
Contract-specific investment			YES				NO			
Ownership of contract-specific assets	Own		Own as tactic to lower barriers to entry and exit	Own as tactic to reduce dependency on supplier				Supplier's decision		
Delivery method being contracted for			Aggregate	Assign / Aggregate				Assemble / Arbitrage		

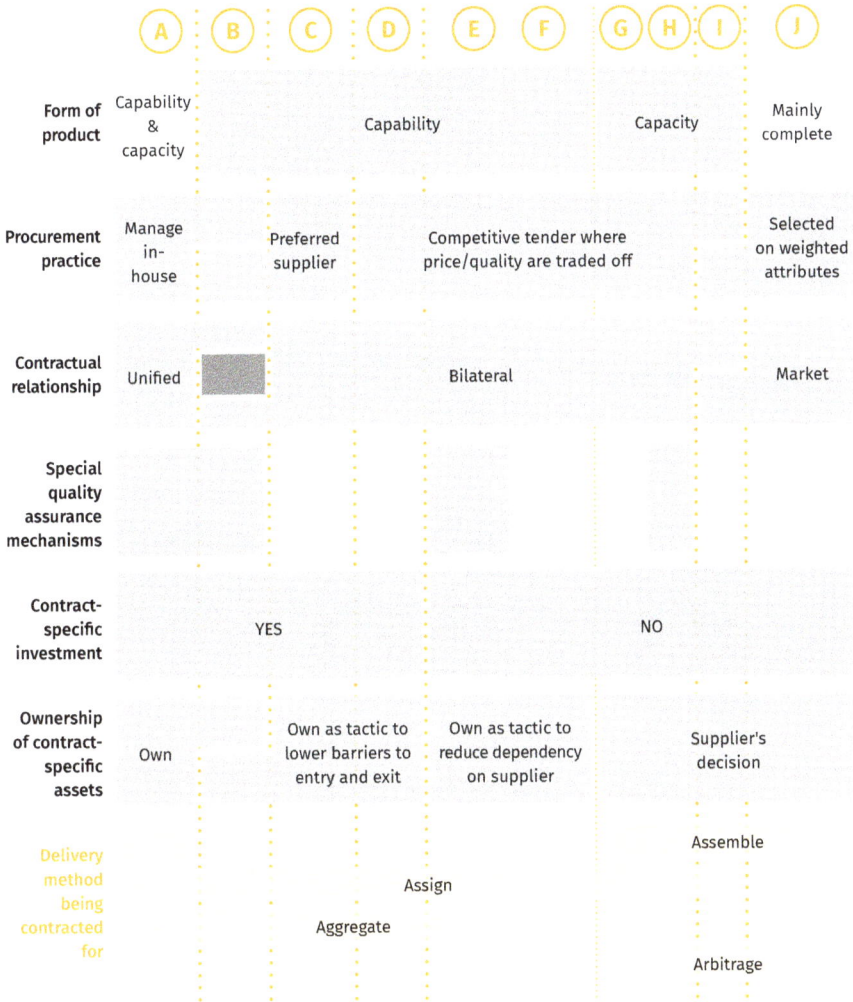

▓ Trilateral may be appropriate here

Method

Facet 6: Production process identified an activity type to create a business angle to exploit the perceived business opportunity, the supporting capabilities and the required knowhow, systems and processes, and other capacities, and their sources. *Figure 19* collates these requirements, together with contextual information on:

› Expected sources, as implied by the activity type chosen (from *Section 6.3: Knowhow, systems & processes*).

› Contract type used in the market (See *Section 3.1: The value network*).

Each of the required knowhow, systems and processes, and other capacity is assessed against the factors that influence the costs and risks of contracting to determine the nature of the contract that can be used – this is done using the decision tree in *Figure 18.* As the scoping business plan may be being developed for a new business angle not seen in the current market – an important finding from this enquiry is whether there are differences, and the reasons for these differences needs to be explained.

This information is used in the next two sections that look at the cost of acquiring and operating planned capabilities. *Figure 19* continues the example being used in previous sections to illustrate this. A variety of contract types are identified, and in all cases, these are consistent with those found in the market and with the activity type.

Figure 19 Deriving the contractual types to acquire capacity

Questions from Figure 18	Knowhow			Systems and process		
	Industry Knowledge	Collaboration platform	Finance & ERP	Fulfullment system	Online store	POS systems
Q1	Only in general terms	Yes	Yes	No because of the functionality required Yes for development platform	No where IP is required to drive website effectiveness	Yes
Q2	No	Yes	Yes	Process engineers can be in short supply Yes for website developers, and development platform	UX designers can be in short supply Yes for website develop-ers, and development platform	Yes
Q3	?	Yes	Yes	No for processes Yes for development platform	No for website Yes for development platform	Yes
Q4	Yes	Yes	Yes	Yes	Yes	Yes
Q5	Only over time, or through catastrophic failure	Yes	Yes	More difficult for fulfilment process Yes for development platform	More difficult for website effective-ness Yes for development platform	Yes
Contract type	Unified	Bilateral or market	Bilateral or market	Unified contract for process designers Bilateral or market for develop-ment platform	Unified contract for UX designers Bilateral or market for develop-ment platform	Bilateral or market
Purchase decsion	Provide in-house	Buy capacity	Buy capacity	Build	Build	Buy capacity

7.2
Cost of systems & processes

Overview

Building on the capabilities identified in *Section 6.3: Knowhow, systems & processes*, the aim of this section is to estimate the cost of acquiring, maintaining and enhancing them.

There are three elements to this:

› the initial cost to acquire scarce resources;

› the cost of maintaining the scarce resource in the face of various forces such as loss of value from

usage, and external factors such as obsolescence; and

› the enhancement of scarce resources. This is a topic discussed in *Section 8.3: Capacity initiatives*.

Note that the discussion here is on the acquisition, maintenance and enhancement of scarce resources, other assets that are not scarce resources are deemed to be operating costs and their ownership is a matter of economic efficiency. One of the objectives of the planning process is to discover the scarce resources that make a business angle valuable.

The analysis is based on free cash flow. Free cash flow analysis is most easily undertaken over the entire lifecycle of a venture. Mid-lifecycle, great care needs to be taken in how the value of scarce resources are maintained as depreciation is not a cash flow, and it is not incorporated into the analysis, but the costs of maintaining the productive capacity of systems and processes must be, and where the cost are insufficient to do this then future profits need to reflect this impairment of the scarce resource.

Method

Having identified the systems and processes, and knowhow underpinning the capability, and the information and communications systems, considerations in estimating their costs and investment required are:

› For each capability, how are the systems and processes to be acquired? If by lease or some usage-based arrangement, then they are an operating cost (these are dealt with in the next section, *Section 7.3: Costs of operating*)?

› What is the driver of additional cost once the system is implemented?

› For the selected solution, what is the expected duration of commitment to it?

› What is the expected price for any resources?

› What is the incremental cost?

› What is the annual maintenance cost so that it reaches its expected life?

› What cost is to be invested to enhance the systems and processes as a scarce resource?

› Are their exit/disposal costs?

Resources that are depleted with use or the passing of time have an initial purchase price, a life expectancy, and a residual value at the end of that life. This residual value can be negative where there are disposal and reinstatement costs at the end-of-life.

Note that the information on operating costs is used in the analysis in the next section, *Section 7.3: Costs of operating.*

7

7.3
Costs of operating

Overview

Continuing the theme of this supplier and partner facet of preparing the scoping plan, the objective is now to estimate the operating costs. To reiterate, costs, in this setting, are cash outflows, and not financial reporting measures and will also be different to the treatment of costs by taxation authorities.

Three types of cost are estimated for each capability:

> Variable costs, those that change with the volume of output

produced. The cost of goods sold is an example of this type of cost.

> Direct costs that are determined by the nature of the business operation. These costs are related, for example, to contractual commitments. Employee salaries and rent can be two costs of this type.

> Other asset costs that are not associated with scarce resources, and contribute to the operation of the business. Note that for financial and taxation reporting these costs are a component of capital expenditure as are some of the costs to acquire scarce resources discussed in the previous section.

Method

Costs are tied to capabilities and costs of a capability are manifested in various functionality. A capability always has a cost for capacity. Depending on the organisational structure adopted and the scope of the capability's activities there are capabilities that are responsible for various assets and liabilities involved in conducting business, such as premises costs, cost of goods sold, inventory, accounts receivable and accounts payable. For each of the application of cash to provide functionality, there is the value of the variable component and the value of the starting position.

What emerges from this analysis are:

› The value of the direct costs that must be met irrespective of the level of sales. Direct costs are fixed cost such as salaries and rent.

› The value of the variable costs that are the cost of goods sold. Examples are products bought for resale and the hire of machinery and machine operators for resale. Variable costs are expressed as the gross margin which is variable cost/revenue.

› The investment that is required in the form of assets, especially the current assets to operate the business. For example, inventories and accounts receivable. Offsetting this are the value of the current liabilities that the business will need to meet, e.g. accounts payable.

The considerations in identifying the costs are:

1. For each of the capacities what is the application of cash to provide functionality:

   › What is the application?

   › What is the determinant of the cost of that application?

   › Is there to be any change in the need for additional expenditure on that application over this planning period?

   › What is the value of the direct costs that must be met irrespective of the level of sales?

   › Should the business grow, what is the unit increase in cost driven by the determinant of cost of the application?

   › What is the contribution of fixed costs to current liabilities?

   › The variable cost for goods sold will be associated with a capability, for that capability:

   › What is the value of the variable costs that are the cost of goods sold?

   › What is the investment that is required in the form of inventories?

   › What is the investment that is required in the form of accounts receivable on the sale of products?

> The value of the current liabilities that the business will need to meet?

2. Other assets and liabilities:

   > Are there any other assets, such as computers and equipment, or liabilities that are required for the functionality?

   > What is the cost of this?

INITIATIVES FOR A SUCCESS-FUL OUTCOME

8

8.1
Success &
assumptions

Overview

Business value depends on:

> Sales to generate income that exceeds cost to breakeven. There are three elements to this, market testing and development, revenue growth, and putting in place mitigants to cover price and sales uncertainty.

> Competitive advantage derived from the creation of core competencies to deliver outputs. For a new venture this involves building capabilities and capacities,

and instituting appropriate mechanisms to mitigate the risks associated with them.

> Investment in knowhow, systems and processes to maintain future earnings.

> Effectiveness in managing a portfolio of salient options that provide business continuity in the face of uncertainty.

Where any matters impacting on these factors are so significant so as to jeopardise the success of the venture, that failure to properly manage them would compromise the success of the venture then they are critical (and are called critical success factors). Adverse impacts in any of these factors could cause the venture to fail, for example, because of:

› Inadequate sales levels and/or realised price.

› Inadequate gross margin as a result of poor operational productivity and/or high cost of inputs.

› Budget overruns, failure to deliver the outcome on time on development and R&D projects.

› Liquidity restrictions due to cash flow and funding problems.

› High cost of accident/disaster – including from liabilities to third parties.

Each of the key considerations needs an explanation of how it is to be managed. They can be managed as part of the 'business as usual' activity of the installed production process; as specific initiatives (discussed in more detail in *Section 8.2: Revenue growth initiatives* and *Section 8.3: Capacity initiatives*); measures instituted to mitigate risks and improve the resilience to meet plans (covered in *Section 8.4: Success & mitigating risks* and *Section 8.5: Resilience & options*); or as part of a general capacity to respond using the knowhow available to the venture (discussed in *Section 6.4: Leadership & key people*). The aim of this enquiry is to set out the key considerations for success, and critical assumptions on which the success of the scoping business plan rests.

Method

The areas critcal to the success of the venture are usually apparent in the analysis in the previous steps. This information is used in the following sections – which set out the ways that will be taken to ensure each critical item is appropriately addressed. In setting out the ways, their costs and benefits are also estimated, and that information is used to compile financial budgets – discussed in *Facet 9: Financial budgets and value.*

In some instances, such as generating demand for a new to market product, no prior information is available, and some risks may be too ambiguous to mitigate. For this, assumptions are made as to their expected outturn,

these are critical assumptions, and their nature is material information for people making decisions on the scoping business plan.

Considerations in identifying the key factors for success of the venture or assumptions being made in the scoping business plan relate to:

› Revenue

› Core competencies

› Future earnings

› Business continuity

8

8.2
Revenue growth initiatives

Overview

Section 5.2: Target revenue established the expected revenue target, and the previous section considered the key areas of success, and critical assumptions, some of which will relate to the potential to realise the target revenues.

The significant effort required to make sales is commonly overlooked and is one of the two key capabilities required by a venture (the other being operational excellence). Sales initiatives require drive and tenacity over a long period of time.

In addition, frequently in the enthusiasm to build a new product the imperative of market testing is often overlooked by new ventures. Revenue targets are therefore tenuous, and with no explanation of how these revenues are to be achieved, the reality is that underlying the business plan is the occurrence of a 'miracle'.

There are three intertwined strands to this enquiry: first, what are the initiatives to realise revenue (and address revenue related key areas of success, and critical assumptions); second, what revenue will these sales initiatives yield (and their timing); and third, what will these sales initiatives cost?

Method

In establishing the expected revenue profile, it is important to tie the initiatives to the achievement of sales levels for the targeted revenue. For example, if the planned revenue is dependent on an advertising campaign then this needs to be described and costed.

Considerations in achieving the planned revenues are:

1. Initiatives that impact on revenue:

›   Which planned initiatives are to drive revenue?

›   What is the nature and timing of that impact?

›   What revenue is expected?

›   What is the cost of the initiatives?

2. Aggregate revenues for each year:

›   Do the revenues from each initiative add up to the planned aggregate revenue?

›   If not, how are the planned revenues to be achieved?

As an example, suppose two key revenue success areas are that:

›   Suitable market segments are identified.

›   Sustained sales and marketing effort.

The first of these requires a programme of actions to substantiate that there is a market for the planned product. With the identification of buyers, then the marketing and sales channels and initiatives are put in place to attain the planned revenue. These initiatives come at a cost.

A rule of thumb that can be used to estimate a revenue growth profile is: a targeted revenue is to be attained at the end of three years and the revenue growth profile follows an S curve. In which, the annual revenue is 10 percent in Year 1 (25 percent of target reached at end of year), 50 percent in Year 2 (50 percent of target reached at end of year), 90 percent in Year 3 (75 percent of target reached at end of year), and 100 percent thereafter. For longer planning periods these S curves from each sales initiative can be added to the previous initiative so that cumulatively the initiatives realise the revenue target.

8

8.3
Capacity initiatives

Overview

The plan to build capacity addresses the timing and investment to put in place the capacity to deliver the functionality required for the venture. For a new venture these are the capabilities and information flows identified in *Section 6.3: Knowhow, systems & processes.*

For an existing enterprise, these initiatives may be part of a business transformation exercise and may be performed by existing capabilities. The aim of this enquiry is to develop a high-level roadmap of the work that must be done, what the work is to contribute to the venture, and its timing and cost.

Method

Capacity enhancement initiatives focus on how the venture's valuable assets are to be enhanced, and the costs and timing of their enhancement. Where assets are to be built or hired, the costs and timing are also explained.

Capacity initiatives draw a distinction between the functionality that is to be performed by the venture's resources, and that which must be managed through supply arrangements. The venture aims to create and enhance its capabilities as valuable core competencies.

Considerations in specifying capacity initiatives are:

› What functionality is to be improved?

› How will this improve the value of the venture?

› What improvement in value is expected?

› What actions are to be improved?

› What is the timing of the actions and realisation of the benefits?

› What resourcing and costs are involved?

8

8.4
Success &
mitigating risk

Overview

Inherent in all commercial activity is uncertainty, some of which can be mitigated. Examples of risk mitigations are: putting in place additional sources of funding, key staff succession arrangements, protecting IP, and purchasing additional capacity.

The starting point of this analysis is the key areas of success identified in *Section 8.1: Success & assumptions*, and the aim of this section is to consider these

identifiable risks, and the mitigants that could be put in place to address them.

Method

The relative contribution of known key success areas can be estimated by the information content they would bring to informing the success of the venture. Information content is measured by the number of surprisals they contribute (a concept used in information theory). A surprisal is the requirement for information gaged by the probability of success – if an outcome is certain (its probability that the outcome will occur is 100%) then its information value is 0, whereas where there is a low probability then there is much to be learned and the surprisal value is high. Surprisals of 1 implies a 50 percent chance of success.

The likelihood of an outcome occurring can be assessed by its odds or probability. Initiatives and risk mitigation actions that improve the likelihood of success can be rated by the improvement made to the probability of achieving the successful outcome. Information Theory measures this improvement in probability as the degree of surprise that the improvement gives – this is quantified in Surprisals. A situation that has odds of 1:1 (50% chance) succeeding is quantified as having -1 Surprisal.

Examples of odds and probability of occurrence and the Surprisal value are:

Odds	Probability	Surprisals
1:1	50.0%	-1
1:3	25.0%	-2
1:7	12.5%	-3
1:15	6.3%	-4
1:31	3.1%	-5

A venture facing multiple areas of high uncertainty without appropriate mitigants has a low probability of success. For example, the average chance of a new business succeeding is about 1 in 100,000 – that is about -17 Surprisals. Management of such a venture would aim to put in place mitigants to ensure success, by making improvements of 17 Surprisals. Suppose the odds of a new venture achieving its sales target is assessed as 1:15 (-4 Surprisals). Recruiting an experienced sales team with contacts in the industry may improve the odds of success to 1:1 (50% probability) – an improvement of 3 Surprisals. The team concluding sales to meet the target revenue provides 1 surprisal in value. Whereas it would be very surprising if the inexperienced sales team were to succeed, they would provide 4 Surprisals on achieving the sales target.

A benefit of calculating surprisals is that they are additive, so the relative impact of different risk mitigants can be compared. Adding the surprisals for each of the key success areas gives the overall, unweighted chance of success. The impact of not finding ways to mitigate the key areas of success is that the venture, in its naïve state, has a low chance of succeeding.

As surprisals are additive, this technique can also be used to estimate the value-for-money impact of alternative mitigation initiatives (using the financial information from *Facet 9: Financial budgets & value*).

Considerations in specifying the actions to promote success are:

› For each facet, what considerations have been identified that are key to the success of the venture? This information is drawn from *Section 8.1: Success & assumptions*.

› For each of the key success areas, what is the probability of success?

- For key success areas with very low probability of success based on current knowledge, what options are available to gain this new knowledge, and do these options give the first best solution?

- For key success areas with very high probability of success based on current knowledge, what is the probability of success (note that there may be interdependencies between the key success areas); and what options are available to protect the first best solution?

- For each identified risk, what is the source of risk; what mitigants are to be used (if any); and what is the cost of the mitigants?

8.5
Resilience
& options

Overview

Businesses build and manage a portfolio of salient strategic options, to provide flexibility to respond to uncertain outturns so as to improve the resilience of achieving plans and budgets.

Managing this portfolio is one of the key roles of management. An example of an option is: where market feedback fails to confirm the market demand, then to quickly respond by reassessing the market and their needs or in extreme cases to close the project – learn fast and act accordingly on that knowledge. The

flexibility to respond may be required in any of the contributors of value. Even where circumstances warrant the use of options, uncertainty will remain around the outturn of plans because future prices are unknown or through miscalculations of market changes; or the knowhow, systems, processes and other arrangements put in place turn out to operate differently to plan; or bad decisions are made. In saying this it should also be recognised that, because of the wide range of uncertain events that might occur, their impact is unknown, and there is high cost of doing something about them, businesses can make no provision for them, instead relying on an overall capacity of the business to respond if the event were to occur. The aim of this examination is to identify areas where steps should be taken to address potential significant positive and negative outturns.

Method

The most commonly used technique for planning the resilience of a business is scenario analysis, which investigates the ramification of an event occurring. The events for these 'what-if' scenarios are drawn from:

› The estimated likelihood of success made in *Section 8.4: Success & mitigating risks*.

› The sensitivities of the key success areas from *Section 9.5: Sensitivities & dependencies*.

› The critical assumptions identified in *Section 8.1: Success & assumptions*.

› The key trends noted in *Section 3.3: Trends & their impact*.

It would be expected that there is strong concordance between the events identified in these various sections.

Where no specific event is identified requiring options to be put in place, options to deal with two scenarios, nonetheless, should be developed:

› the off-ramps if the project fails to live up to expectations; and

› the next stage in the project lifecycle if the project succeeds.

Appraising Business Opportunities

FINANCIAL BUDGETS & VALUE

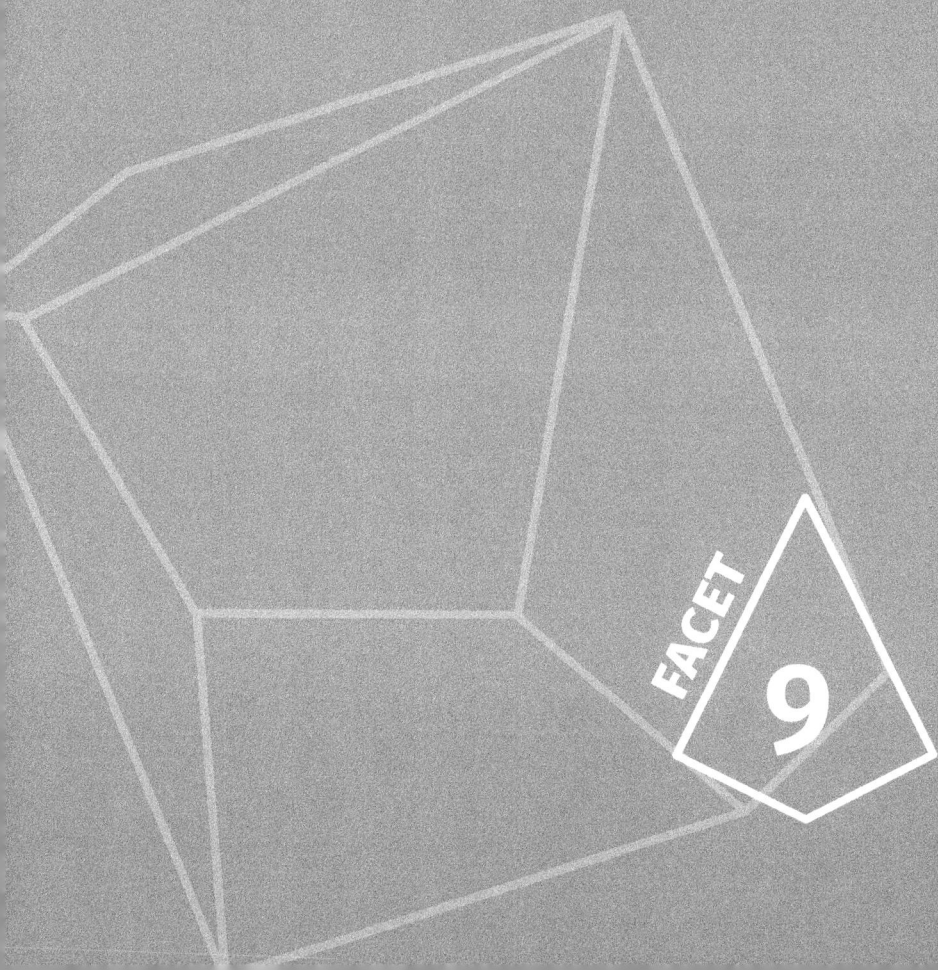

9.1
Financial budgets

Overview

Financial budgets bring together estimates made of revenue, operating costs, investment in systems and processes and working capital, and the timing of this investment. This information is used to estimate profitability, and the requirements for cash and funding from shareholders and other providers of finance.

Method

In compiling the scoping plan information is prepared on:

> The sources of funding and its cost (from *Facet 2: Aims, resources & constraints*).

> Target Revenue (from *Section 5.2: Target revenue*).

> Gross margin which is variable cost/price (from *Section 7.3: Costs of operating*)

> Other operating costs (from *Section 7.3: Costs of operating*)

> Expected expenditure on systems and processes (from *Section 7.2: Cost of systems & processes*).

› Planned development costs and revenue profile (from *Facet 8: Initiatives for a successful outcome*).

› Projected lifespan of the project (from *Facet 2: Aims, resources & constraints*).

Financial information is structured into the following parts:

A. Revenue and operating expenses.

B. Investment in systems and processes.

C. Investment in working capital.

D. Cash flow position.

Where a venture has a short lifespan, then the entire lifespan can be estimated. Where the venture is expected to have an on-going life, then budgets can be prepared for a three to five year period.

The first two of these parts (A and B) combine information that has already been prepared in earlier sections. Working capital is the investment (Part C) required to run the business such as to invest in inventories, pay commitments (such as salaries, rent and suppliers) and promises by customers to pay for their purchases. More precisely, as a word equation:

| Working capital | = | Current assets | − | Current liabilities |

Examples of current assets are cash, accounts receivable, inventories and other assets that can be easily liquidated. Current liabilities include accounts payable.

Part D calculates the cash position separately from that of the other working capital items. This is because the venture needs sufficient cash to meet its obligations as they fall due. If there is insufficient cash, then additional funding must be found in the form of new funds from shareholders or increased borrowings. The converse of this is that surplus cash can be used to repay shareholders or long-term lenders. The funding considerations are covered in part D.

Returning to part C, to estimate budgets, a rule-of-thumb is that all expenses are paid in the month (the accounts payable) in which they are incurred. Cash sales are received in the month of the sale, whereas invoiced sales are collected (accounts receivable) in the month following sale. Another rule-of-thumb is to estimate the investment in inventory as one quarter to one third of the annualised end of year sales revenue.

Whereas, part D shows the net cash position. It takes the cash income and deducts the cash outflows. Some of these cash flows are associated with the investment in systems and processes, working capital and operating activities. Some is from cash transfers to and from shareholders and borrowings from lenders. These cash transfers must meet the cash flow requirements of operating the venture, such that the cash contributions are sufficient to achieve a positive cash balance over the entire budget period. Where borrowings are to be used as a source of cash, then the interest charge must be subtracted as a use of cash. The interest charge is calculated as the average borrowings (that is one half of the borrowings at the start of the year plus one half the borrowings at the end of the year) multiplied by the interest rate (part of the information gathered in *Section 9.4: Discount rate*).

Tax should also be provided for in the application of cash (having said this, financial budgets prepared for corporate projects usually exclude tax). The calculation of tax is subject to its own legislation and varies between jurisdictions. Estimate of the tax payment is calculated in *Section 9.2: Financial reports*.

9

9.2
Financial reports

Overview

Financial information on ventures is presented in the form of reports that conform to generally accepted accounting practice (GAAP), meeting accounting standards, and companies, tax and other legislative requirements.

Preparation of these reports is usually required when seeking external investment. In-house projects usually rely on the cash flow analysis, presented above, and do not need the development of financial reports.

Method

For a scoping plan, much of the information prepared for cash based financial budgets (*Section 9.1: Financial budgets*) is used to prepare the financial reports. The key difference is that financial reports prepared by following GAAP show the legal obligations between the venture and other parties including customers, suppliers, lenders, shareholders and tax agencies. The Profit and Loss Statement summarise the financial transactions that take place over the course of a financial year, while the Balance Sheet shows the assets, liabilities and owners equity at the start and end of the financial year. The important implication to note between these two different points of view in preparing financial information is that cash flow recognises the timing of the receipts and expenditure of cash whereas the information prepared under GAAP recognises obligations – and where the flow of cash is different from the obligations then adjustments are incorporated into the GAAP prepared reports. For example, sales on account that are paid the month following end of month invoicing are recognised in the Profit and Loss Statement in the month in which the sale is made whereas the cash is received in the following month. The financial accounting adjustments are called accruals.

Additional items that are calculated for the Profit and Loss Statement are:

> Depreciation is a method of allocating the cost of tangible assets over their useful life. Amortisation refers to the allocation of the cost of intangible assets such as goodwill over their useful life.

> Corporate tax.

Both these items are determined by tax legislation and other reporting standards, and will need to be ascertained. Tax authorities make this information readily available.

The Balance Sheet comprises three components, that are related in the following way:

Assets = Liabilities + Owner's equity

Assets are categorised into current and non-current assets. Current assets are calculated in the previous section on the cash flow information. Non-current assets cover the investment made in items such as building, plant, equipment, hardware and software less the accumulated depreciation.

Assets are funded by liabilities, such as through borrowings and cash contributed by shareholders. Shareholder contributions can be as shareholder advances (a liability) or paid up capital and recorded as owners equity. Where all assets, liabilities and shareholders paid in capital are properly accounted for, the balance sheet equation is brought into balance through the owners equity item: retained earnings. As the name suggests the change in the retained earnings is the net profit for the year.

For a scoping business plan, the financial reports (Balance Sheet and Profit and Loss Statement) are a re-presenation of the financial information collected in *Section 9.2: Financial budgets*

9.3
Lifespan & value

Overview

Market opportunities have a lifespan, for example, for spontaneous opportunities the lifespan is short, whereas, many ventures are established with the expectation that the opportunity will be on-going.

Aside from the alignment of the expected lifespan with the aim of the venture, at the analytical level the remaining life at the end of the planning period will determine the method of valuing the terminal value of the project. The aim of this section is to estimate the FCF value of the venture.

Valuing ventures is a complex matter with many nuanced methodological and practical considerations. In the context of constructing a high-level scoping business plan, the need is for tools that provide an indication of whether a project has some prospect of being profitable. The two methods described here are chosen for their simplicity, but with simplicity comes significant assumptions. This sensitivity of the valuation calculation to the assumptions being made is easily demonstrated by the impact of small changes in discount and growth rate assumptions on the resultant FCF value. Be mindful that the valuation methods here are no more than indicators of the profitability of a venture for a scoping plan.

1. Project with planned end-of-life

Projects with planned end-of-life are valued as the net present value of the cashflows over the entire life of the project. The present value is calculated using the discount rate discussed in *Section 9.4: Discount rate*. The terminal value is the disposal value of the assets at the end of the venture less the liabilities that must be settled.

2. Projects that are expected to continue to grow

For projects where there is an expectation that the business will be on-going, the terminal value can be estimated using a variation of the Gordon growth model. As an equation the model is:

$$\text{Terminal value} = \text{Expected future revenue} \times \frac{\text{Profit after allowances}}{\text{Revenue}} \times \frac{1 + \text{After-allowances margin growth rate}}{\text{Discount rate} - \text{After-allowances margin growth rate}}$$

The FCF margin is residual profit after funding the investment in systems and processes, and working capital. The FCF margin to revenue growth rate is the projected growth rate in the relative margin. Its value is zero where no change in FCF margin to revenue is anticipated. The valuation is highly sensitive to this growth rate, and given the structure of the growth model its value must be less than the discount rate.

Method

Where a venture has a short lifespan, then the entire lifespan can be depicted in the key cash flow budgets and the net present value of the venture is calculated using the discount rate. Where the venture is expected to have an on-going life, the modified Gordon growth model is used to calculate the terminal value.

For this, the following are required:

> Target revenue (estimated in *Section 5.2: Target revenue*).

> Discount rate (established in *Section 9.4: Discount rate*).

> FCF margin.

> Rate of growth in the FCF margin.

Appraising Business Opportunities

The FCF margin is devised to incorporate the investment in systems and processes etc. that a venture needs to make overtime to preserve or enhance them to support the projected income earning ability of the venture. In many business settings, such as those involving a high degree of change and uncertainty, the depreciation rate used for tax purposes is a poor approximation of the on-going investment requirement. It is for this reason that it is suggested that the FCF margin is used. This is to ensure that the on-going requirements in assets and working capital are incorporated into the valuation. The FCF margin is the FCF profit less:

› increase in working capital; and

› change in capital expenditure.

The rate of growth in the FCF margin is the measure of the ability to continuously increase the FCF margin, for example because the venture develops core competencies that will continuously, over a long period of time increase the after allowances margin. This estimation of this rate of growth requires projections to be made beyond the planning period. Where the margin is not expected to change the rate of growth is zero, and where it is expected to fall, for example because of the impact of competition, then it is negative.

The estimate of the terminal value is then added to the final year estimate of the Free Cash Flow to Equity – the rationale for this is that were the project to be sold at that point in time, it would realise the estimated terminal value as its sale price.

Applying the discount rate (from *Section 9.4: Discount rate*) to the estimated yearly cash flow plus terminal value and then summing the result gives the estimate of the FCF value of the project.

9

9.4
Discount rate

Overview

The discount rate is the compensation investors expect for the commitment of funds to the venture. Considerations in formulating this compensation are:

> Uncertainty and risk involved associated with the future cashflows.

> Period that funds are committed.

> Competition between lenders.

> Expected inflation during the commitment period.

Method

The discount rate is expressed as the required rate of return investors expect for the commitment of funds.

A range of sources are used to gather the required data:

> For internal projects, the discount rate is commonly estimated as the prevailing interest rate available to the business, for example as the business borrowing interest rate that could be accessed by the venture. The justification for using this is that it is an estimate of the opportunity cost (forgone net benefit) faced by the investors (as the underwriter of the loan) in this type of business. For business

valuations, this is a poor proxy of the discount rate.

› The term of stakeholders' participation in the venture and conditions under which they will exit it, is also required. Usually, it is quite clear to stakeholders the term and conditions for their continued involvement in a project.

9

9.5
Sensitivities & dependencies

Overview

Business plans and budgets do not usually identify the revenue and costs associated with options, and the resilience to cope with the occurrence of uncertain events.

Specific questions about the overall impact of option and uncertainty premiums that need answering are:

› has the venture any prospect of generating positive FCF value given uncertainty about the estimates of sales, margin, fixed costs and capital expenditure; and

› with any variation in these areas of uncertainty, what impact does this have on the need for capital investment?

Method

Scenario models and sensitivity analysis are used to gage the impact of variations in variables such as attaining sales targets and capital budget overruns on the value of, and need for further investment in the venture. Both these factors are important as they may cause stakeholders to withdraw their support for the venture.

Sensitivity can be calculated by applying a small percentage change to a variable then calculating the percentage change in value and capital requirement. Where information is available, variations in variables can be assigned a probability of occurrence, and the likely outcome and range of outcomes calculated. Sensitivity analysis is also performed on the impact of the initiatives, risk mitigants and options selected in *Facet 8: Initiatives for a successful outcome*.

As an example, suppose the analysis of risks in *Section 8.4: Success & mitigating risks* has already established that for this venture, the unweighted probability of success is about 50 percent. Confronting this challenge, might see the imperative of monitoring key indicators of performance of:

› achieving and exceeding sales targets, followed closely by attaining and exceeding the planned gross margin; and

› ensuring that gross margin and fixed costs are within budget.

Failure to achieve these should provide alarm signals that the planned for value of the venture may not be attainable.

As another example, suppose two scenarios are appropriate:

› Base case of meeting plan – 50% probability giving a project with FCF value after three years of $23 million for an outlay of $1.2 million.

› Undershoot case, in which the venture fails – 50% probability with a loss of more than $1.5 million, in which the off-ramp set out in *Section 8.5: Resilience & options* would be activated.

Even with these probabilities, the project is worth undertaking as the expected value is some $12 million.

As a side note, estimates of sensitivity can be used to develop weightings for use in the analysis in *Section 8.4: Success & mitigating risks.*

Without a clear understanding of the risks and their drivers, and the translation of this understanding into plans and key performance indicators, the exit cost could be much higher.

ASSESS-MENT OF THE ANALYSIS

FACET

10

▲ 10

10.1
Realism of the plan

Overview

The purpose of the assessment of this scoping plan is to provide confidence that the business angle identified is an opportunity with some commercial merit, even if at this point in the planning process its feasibility and viability have still to be assessed.

Evaluations are made of the utility of evidence used, methods have been applied appropriately to it, and the overall conclusions reached are sound. One of the outputs from the

scoping plan is to identify gaps in information which could improve the uncertainty associated with the high-level assessment of the plan.

Method

There are two aspects to the assessment. First is the thoughtful application of the analytical tools to yield useful information, both individually and in its entirety. For the overall assessment, gaps in information that could reduce uncertainty about the perceived business opportunity. Second, that the limitations of the available information are acknowledged in the analysis. The findings from the assessment help form a view on the timing, riskiness of pursuing the perceived opportunity, and the gaps in information that could reduce uncertainty about the value of the opportunity.

The coverage of the evaluation of the individual analyses is:

› Are the key considerations identified?

› Does each depiction in the analytical tool concur with reality?

› Are gaps in information and assumptions set out?

› Are the content and conclusions of the analytical tool documented?

The evaluation of the overall conclusions reached, encompassing:

› Do the conclusions from each stage link together in a logical manner?

› Does the overall analysis produce meaningful results?

› Is the timeframe of the window to grasp the perceived opportunity outlined?

› Are there practical means to monitor changes in the assessment of the perceived opportunity, especially in the form of information from market testing, and the availability of new information that could fill in gaps in the available information base?

› If the key variables and assumptions were to change are the impacts plausible?

As a rule, each claim about the reason for the existence of the perceived opportunity must be substantiated with evidence. Where the claim is not supported, the proposition is revised. Where through repeated testing, the evidence still does not support the claim, then the business angle needs to be discarded or at least seriously rethought. This process is not without its problems. For this, the one-page-summary can be a useful tool to quickly incorporate new knowledge into the analysis.

The opportunity analysis (*Facet 1: The business opportunity*) has as one of the factors influencing the statement of the opportunity the degree to which the scope relates to a specific area or generic to this type of area. A subtle influence which can lead to an overestimation of the size of the opportunity is 'scope creep' that can infect the analysis as the scope of the opportunity is adjusted to fit the available data, depending on the element market at the centre of the opportunity.

A more serious problem is that the evaluation cannot address knowledge deficiencies where the planner 'doesn't know what they don't know'. To tackle that problem access to people with the appropriate subject matter knowledge is necessary.

It is important for this scoping business planning exercise to be able to identify low cost ways of sourcing information to provide evidence. This may involve running in-market experiments and constructing prototypes to gather information. In product markets, purchase orders from potential customers are the best form of information on the demand for the planned product. Without this evidence, the scoping study runs a high risk of manufacturing a result founded in desk research myopia.

10

10.2
Market-centric evaluation process

This guide describes an approach to evaluating the rationality of a perceived business opportunity by considering it from the point of view of the five element markets in which it must thrive.

The approach is to form a coherent picture of how the business opportunity will be realised through a business angle to flourish in each element market. The evaluation in the scoping business plan is like a 10 sided prism, each facet providing a different insight on the opportunity from an external market vantage point.

Facet 1: The business opportunity

starts by articulating the perceived business opportunity that is to be evaluated. This is the anchor for the rest of the analysis.

Financial markets

Consideration of financial markets starts with establishing the expectations for the venture and the financial and other resources available to it. This is set out in Facet 2 Aims, resources and constraints. Working with these, financial market considerations are framed in terms of the expected cash flows. First, whether the available resources are sufficient to support financial viability. Second, where the venture is viable to estimate its value using the FCF method. For this, in addition to estimates of the cash flows, information on the venture's lifespan and the prevailing discount rate are required. The discount rate is an estimate of the opportunity cost of undertaking this venture. The discount rate provides a direct link to the alternative uses of capital, while the FCF value gauges whether the venture has any prospect of creating core competencies that might be attractive to others. These considerations are traversed in *Facet 9: Financial budgets & value.*

Value network from the nature of the value network and how it is expected to change. The production process is the second component of the business angle. *Facet 6: Production process* develops the full description of the production process. The selection of a production process is linked to asset markets through the drive to create core competencies. This is developed in the description of the selection of activity type; knowhow, systems and processes; and the contribution of leadership and key people.

Product markets

A high level description of the product market is provided in the description of the value network in which the venture is to operate, and the trends at work changing its shape – set out in *Facet 3: Place the opportunity.* This is to ground the perceived opportunity into the need to find a place in the market. From this starting point, *Facet 4: Buyers & the friction they face* investigates the target buyer, the customer journey, and customers' view on the product attributes. Firmly rooting this in the market for this product, *Facet 5: Demand, alternatives & competition* clarifies where the product is placed compared to competitors, and from this the revenue expectations. This is one of the two components in formulating the business angle.

Commodity markets

The description of the value network in *Facet 3: Value network* provides the context for the commodity market that the venture is to operate in. *Facet 7: Suppliers & partners* describes the nature of inputs to be purchased and their costs, and the contractual relationships to be established with suppliers in the market.

Market for other contractual commitments

The market for other contractual commitments relates to the use of contracts to manage obligations to other parties. Key objectives include ensuring resilience and plans are met, certain outcomes are mitigated such as those related to health and safety; and environmental impact. *Facet 8: Initiatives for a successful outcome* does this by addressing these concerns related to: assumptions made about the proposition; realising

Asset markets

Some information on the variety of production processes used by competitors can be gleaned in *Facet 3:*

revenue growth initiatives; delivering capacity building initiatives; mitigating risk; and off-ramps.

Facets of the scoping business plan elucidate the perceived opportunity from the perspectives of each element market and from these multiple views to form a conclusion on the expected value of the opportunity. Embedding market considerations into the evaluation process this this a market centric planning process. This is the central proposition, that the evaluation of a perceived business opportunity must consider each of the multiple element markets.

Key influences on the work

The business angle as a concept to understand an implementable business opportunity is developed by Robert Hughes in *The Drive of Business: Strategies for Creating Business Angles*, published in 2016. This book is an application guide to implementing that concept. The frameworks described in this book draw on the consulting assignments of Hughes Consulting Limited which have implemented these frameworks in multiple assignments.

Other notable influences include *Principles of Economics* by Alfred Marshall, first published in 1890 on the use of the demand curve to depict market relationships.

Oliver Williamson's papers 'Transaction-Cost Economics: The Governance of Contractual Relations' in a 1979 edition of *Journal of Law and Economics*; and 'Strategizing, Economizing, and Economic Organisation' in *Strategic Management* published in 1991 on the economics of contracting.

Jay Barney's 2001 paper on core competencies and their value to a business 'Is the resource-based 'view' a useful perspective for strategic management research? Yes' published in *Academy of Management Review*.

Aswath Damodaran provides a full account of the FCF method of valuation in *Investment Valuation: Tools and techniques for determining the value of any asset*, first published in 1996.

GLOSSARY

Activity type

Activity type is the specific method used in the production process to transform acquired inputs into delivered outputs.

Addressable market

The addressable market is the customers that can be reached by the organisation.

Aggregate method

Aggregate method provides products by operate capabilities using the knowhow, systems and processes that depend on the law of large numbers and scale-free infrastructure networks.

Arbitrage method

Arbitrage method applies knowhow, systems, and processes to identify differences in the price of products and resources that are caused by asymmetries in information and high transaction cost. This method relies on transaction specific knowledge, which can arise from barriers to information, location, time, customer relationships, etc.

Assemble method

Assemble method uses knowhow, systems, and processes to produce products by exploiting economies of scale and scope.

Asset

1. Assets are products with positive value that the organisation has rights of ownership or control.

2. Assets are stocks of benefits and include tangible assets (e.g. land, building, machinery, tools, and inventory) and intangible assets (e.g. goodwill, patents, working capital and bank accounts). Assets may not have a market value and are recorded in the Balance Sheet following GAAP.

Assign method

Assign method produces products using knowhow, systems, and processes to operate capabilities that gain efficiencies by improving coordination, by ensuring close alignment of the interests between principals and agents.

Bandwagon effect

Bandwagon effect is a social network effect that occurs when demand increases with more users, for example, phone networks attract more users as usage increases.

Bargaining power

The ability to dictate the allocation of value added.

Benefit

Benefit is derived from product attributes that can be real, service attributes and include intangible benefits from product meaning, brand association, fashion, and bandwagon effects, to name a few.

Brand

Brand refers to notoriety and reputation. Positive brand can be associated with ease of access to buyers and providers, lower transaction costs, increased transactions, and higher margins. Brand is frequently equated to a person, product, organisation, or idea.

Business angle

A business angle is a perceived opportunity and an activity type to exploit it.

Business model

The business model is the way in which the business opportunity is converted into profit. This covers the activity type including its knowhow, systems and processes, organisational structure, product specifications, and target buyers.

Business opportunity

Business opportunity is an intervention in a market to potentially earn profit.

Business proposition

A business proposition is a description of the business opportunity with the supporting business model to exploit it.

Capability

Capabilities utilise resources and supporting information through the application of knowhow, systems, and processes to perform actions that contribute to the functions of an organisation. Capabilities and supporting information contribute to the methods used to acquire inputs and deliver products.

Capacity

Capacity is the output volume that can be produced by a capability with its supporting information. Capacity is limited by knowhow, systems, and processes to perform functional actions and input resources.

Capital

Capital is the funds provided by lenders and investors. The price of capital from lenders is the interest rate charged. The return to investors is a share of profits such as dividends.

Commodities

Commodities are consumed in production processes. Commodities include resources such as labour effort, electricity, and leases on property. Commodities are usually purchased using market and bilateral contracts.

Competitive advantage

Competitive advantage is the value that is attributed to scarce resources and is measured by FCF value. High competitive advantage is associated with high FCF value of scarce resources – which incorporate the ability to generate profits in the future – for the expected sales.

Contractual commitments

Contractual commitments is a catchall category for items that arise from express terms and conditions between the parties to an agreement, sometimes in the form of a legally binding agreement and which are not otherwise classified as commodities and assets. Contractual commitments are intertwined with the organisation's dealings in all element markets. Importantly contractual claims can create assets as well as liabilities for the organisations. These contracts can be bilateral or trilateral. GAAP and tax authorities have specific rules for the treatment of some contractual commitments.

Contributors of value

There are five contributors that can improve FCF value. They do this by: improving the value-for-money of products that leads to improved revenue (Contributor 1); improving the selection and purchase of inputs that result in lower input costs (Contributor 2); improving the productivity and effectiveness of the production process to enhance scarce resources (Contributor 3); improving the use of appropriate risk mitigants to ensure that business plans are met, and improving the use of strategic options to extend the on-going profitability of the organisation (Contributor 4); and improving financial management so that it adds to the value of the organisation (Contributor 5).

Coordination mechanism

Products are exchanged according to the coordination mechanisms used between the parties. There are four types of coordination mechanism. Push/push coordination involves the supplier producing products as a precursor to offering them for sale in the market. Push/pull coordination is the production for inventory, that is subsequently drawn down by buyers, or where capacity or capability are put in place to be called on when required. Pull/pull relates to customised production when a product is produced to meet a custom order. Pull/push production is contract production for a buyer's inventory, from which the buyer then draws down their requirements.

Core competency

A core competency is a capability or set of capabilities with supporting information that contribute to the creation of positive FCF value for the organisation.

Critical assumptions

Critical assumptions are known uncertainties about the business model and market context that are required to be true for the planned outturn to be realised.

Critical success factor

The attainment of a state necessary to achieve the planned outcome is a critical success factor.

Declining cost economies

Declining cost economies are positive feedback effects that create value added through lower average costs, increasing barriers to entry or lower transaction costs, and include those derived from size, scale and scope achieved in the operation of knowhow, systems, and processes; agency costs, the law of large numbers, scale-free infrastructure networks and density economies; asymmetries in access to information, knowledge, institutional arrangements, and location and time.

Demand curve

A demand curve shows the relationship between price and the quantity of a product bought.

Element markets

The element markets are the range of different markets in which an organisation operates, which includes the markets for products, commodities, assets, financial assets, and contractual commitments.

Expected profit

Expected profit is the planned for profit based on estimates of income, less costs including the premiums for uncertainty and options.

FCF

Free cash flow – see *profit*.

FCF value

FCF value is calculated as the net present value of expected future free cash flows.

Feedback effects

Feedback effects refer to the nature of the interrelationship between the attainment of one state (e.g. volume produced) and value of another state (e.g. cost structure). Feedback effects can be supply and demand-side effects and the impact can be positive, negative, or neutral. For example, with the production of more output the impact of positive feedback is declining average costs and negative feedback would result in increasing average costs.

Friction

Another term for transaction cost.

GAAP

Generally Accepted Accounting Principles.

Gross margin

Gross margin is profit to sales revenue (ProfitSales) expressed as a percentage.

Information

Information covers data, details, facts, and knowledge about a situation.

Information asymmetries

Information asymmetries refer to situations where one party has better information than others and this causes the parties to behave differently. Information asymmetries arise from constraints on access to data, deficiencies in knowledge, from institutional arrangements, from geographic location, and because of time.

Inputs

In the setting of the definition of profit, an input is any cash expenditure such as on commodities and assets.

Institutional arrangements

Institutional arrangements cover, for instance, social conventions, the law, and agreements.

Investment

The commitment of assets, including capital, resources, labour (such as in sweat equity) and reputation to an organisation.

Knowhow

Knowhow is the domain specific expertise and experience that can be applied to specified capabilities to profit from scarce resources and speculation.

Law of large numbers

The phenomenon where, with more occurrences of an unconnected event, the occurrence of an event lies more closely to the average occurrence of the event.

Market

A market is the institutions, social conventions, infrastructure, and capabilities that facilitate the repeated exchange of products, assets, skills, capital, information, and other resources.

Market context

Market context is an umbrella term for the situation that applies to a particular market, including its size, suppliers and buyers, the products, and societal expectations, institutional arrangements, and cultural norms in which it operates.

Market disruption

A market disruption is a buyer experience that occurs when comparative value-for-money changes rapidly enough to be noteworthy, forcing a re-evaluation of spending patterns.

Market positioning strategies

Strategies used by organisations to carve out a place in a value network for their products. These market segmentation strategies stem from: cost (Position 1), domain (Position 2), extemporaneous (Position 3), segmentation (Position 4), shared transaction costs (Position 5), and captive market (Position 6).

Market value

Market value is the price obtained for a product or asset in a fair sale. When applied to the business it is the value of the business as a going concern.

Method

Method is a set of capabilities with supporting information enabling the acquisition of inputs or delivery of outputs.

Opportunity cost

The opportunity cost is the net benefit forgone by pursuing the best alternative course of action.

Option

An option confers the right, but not an obligation, to undertake a certain course of events. A tradeable option contract involves the purchaser of the option paying a fee for the right to buy (called a call option) or sell (this is a put option) a real or financial asset at a specified price. A real option is the right but not the obligation to undertake some real business activity. Unlike tradable option contracts, real options, in general, cannot be traded as securities and may not be precisely time bound. The term option is used in two ways:

1. Strategic options which provide the capacity to respond to uncertain events so as to provide on-going continuity for the organisation.

2. Tactical options that address short term variations due to events such as price fluctuations.

Organisation

Organisation refers to any entity engaged in economic activity to exploit a business angle. In this setting, an organisation can be a business unit within an existing corporate, a new start-up venture, consortium, joint venture, or a businessperson operating on their own account. An organisation may or may not be constituted as a legal entity, such as a limited liability company or cooperative society, charity, amongst other forms.

Organisational structure

The organisational structure refers to knowledge acquisition, business strategy, organisational architecture, and incentive schemes.

Outputs

In the setting of the definition of profit, an output is any cash income, most importantly products. Some outputs are inputs that are resold.

Participants

Participants are involved with an organisation and in a value network, including buyers, providers, suppliers, competitors, and government.

Parties

Parties are the participants in a transaction that involve contractual claims, such as buyers and their suppliers, and principals and agents. For example, there are parties to a contract and participants in a market.

Perceived benefit

The benefits to the buyer including aspirational benefits in the form of its product meaning, such as its allure within the culture and context in which the product is offered for sale.

Preference curve

The value-for-money relationship between price and perceived benefit is depicted by the preference curve.

Principal

See explanation for agents. A buyer is a principal.

Product

Product is used as a generic term for items that are exchanged between parties in product markets and have attributes that provide benefits such as service quality.

Product meaning

Product meaning refers to how buyers relate to a product because of connotations associated with its physical, functional, symbolic, and cultural attributes.

Production process

The production process is the overarching term for the collection of capabilities and supporting information used by the organisation. A production process has organisational structure, activity type that uses production technology with appropriate knowhow, systems and processes, resources, and contractual obligations to transform a volume of inputs into outputs.

Profit

Profit during a period is the net operating profit after tax, less the change in working capital and expenditure required to maintain the operating profit. This definition of profit is also known as free cash flow. An approximation of free cash flow from the financial accounts of a business is EBIT (1 – tax rate) plus depreciation and amortization less change in working capital less expenditure to maintain the current operating capability.

Profit margin

Profit margin is the ratio of profit to sales revenue.

Resource

A resource is a source or supply of profit. To illustrate this concept, whereas real estate property is an asset, the flow of benefits it provides (e.g. shelter, prestige) is a resource. The asset can be sold. By letting real estate the resource is sold. Other examples of resources are labour effort and knowhow.

Risk

1. The variation from the target value that is anticipated, and its consequences assessed. Risk is management's expectation of the variation, but is only one component of uncertainty. Before the event it is impossible to know the degree to which risk is aligned to the uncertainty.

2. Synonym for uncertainty, connoting exposure to loss which, for example, could result in loss of capital invested.

Scale-free infrastructure networks

Scale-free infrastructure networks relates to production processes, especially infrastructure networks, which involve high initial fixed cost and diminishing unit costs, and which follow a power law relationship for the addition of more users.

Scarce resources

Scarce resources are distinguished from other assets by their price being established by their profit earning ability. Scarce resources include core competencies and can include physical assets, financial assets, and legal rights.

Speculation

Speculation is the act of picking a future price for a product or asset.

Spontaneous industries

Spontaneous industries are short-lived clusters of organisations in a locality centred on a single industry that emerge where conditions are conducive and last for only as long as those conditions persist.

Stage

Value networks are broken in stages by markets. A stage comprises capabilities organised into one or more nodes.

Strategy

A set of directed actions to realise an objective. A surprisal is the logarithm (to base 2) of the probability of occurrence.

Surprisal

Measure of the degree of surprise that new information or an improvement gives. A situation that has odds of 1:1 (50% chance) succeeding is quantified as having -1 Surprisals, whereas odds of 1:3 (25% chance) is -2 Surprisals.

System

1. A network of capabilities and information flows with resultant behaviour responses to external stimuli. In this meaning an organisation is a system, as is a value network.

2. The equipment, software, plant, machinery, infrastructure, and procedures used in processes following prescribed procedures, which provide the capability and capacity to deliver an organisation's outputs, for example a computer system.

Transaction costs

The costs incurred in the process of organisations transacting are transaction cost. These include searching, negotiating, changes to be able to use the product, ambiguity in scope of the product being contracted for, monitoring performance, invoicing and payment, maintaining documentation and performance failure.

Uncertainty

Uncertainty is the variation from the target value. Uncertainty ranges from risk (that is, the known unknowns in which the likelihood of events occurring can be assessed); through to acknowledgement of unknown knowns, for example, severe rare events where the potential for occurrence is recognised even though their occurrence may be unknown; and on through to unknowable events. These events can occur in all contributors to business value and cover uncertainty in price, opportunity, input, capability, decision, business value, and regulatory and institutional arrangements.

Value

That is business value of FCF value – see *FCF value*.

Value added

Value added is the difference between the benefit enjoyed by buyers from a product less the cost to produce it. Value added is the sum of the value-for-money to buyers plus the profit to suppliers.

Value network

Value network is a network of capabilities and supporting information, usually from more than one organisation, which culminates in the capacity to deliver products to the final consumer.

Value network map

A value network map is a depiction of the stages in a value network, the participants at each stage as measured by their market share, and the relationship between the participants.

Value proposition

Value proposition is the promise that a product will deliver perceived benefits to the buyer for the price.

Value-for-money

Value-for-money is the difference between the perceived benefit to the buyer of a product and its price.

Value-for-money indifference curve
The value-for-money indifference curve describes the relationship between price and the perceived benefit of the product.

www.ingramcontent.com/pod-product-compliance
Lightning Source LLC
Chambersburg PA
CBHW040927210326
41597CB00030B/5212